50 Tales of Flight

From Biplanes to Boeings.

By

Owen Zupp

First published in 2013.

Registered Office P.O. Box 747, Bowral NSW 2576. Australia.

Author: Zupp, Owen 1964-

Title: 50 Tales of Flight. From Biplanes to Boeings.

Owen Zupp

ISBN: 978-0-9874954-3-3

Subjects: Aeroplanes. Piloting.-Biography. Air pilots,-Australia

Also by Owen Zupp.

"50 More Tales of Flight"

"Solo Flight" An Aviation Adventure.

"The Practical Pilot." A Pilot's Common Sense Guide to Safer Flying.

"Down to Earth" A Fighter Pilot's Experiences of surviving Dunkirk, the Battle of Britain, Dieppe and D-Day. (Grub Street Publishing. 2007)

Author's Website. www.owenzupp.com and www.thepilotsblog.com

Contents

Images

1. In the Jabiru on my way around Australia
2. The Boeing 737-800 at Dusk
3. The cause of the "Big Bang". A separated cylinder head on my Cessna 210
4. The impressive N3N, complete with 'planter' at Chino, California
5. A QANTAS Airbus A380 on its final approach to land
6. Seven young men. Selwyn Booth and his Pathfinder crew
7. Wallaby Airlines. A Royal Australian Air Force Caribou in Vietnam
8. If These Walls Could Speak. The cockpit of Kingsford-Smith's 'Southern Cross'
9. Does it get any better than this? A Piper Cub on a summer's afternoon
10. 'Jabiru Dawn' at Kalbarri, Western Australia
11. Squadron Leader Kenneth Butterworth McGlashan AFC
12. Joie De Vivre! The scarlet Stearman over the waves
13. Flight Testing the Cozy Mark IV
14. The Mustang
15. Refuelling the Tiger Moth. Old School
16. Flying Officer Robert Bruce Eggins. Killed in Action 4th March 1945
17. Kenneth McGlashan's Hawker Hurricane on the beach at Dunkirk in 1940 and 1988.
18. An impressive contrail as an aircraft ahead turns for home at the end of the day
19. Dad

***

Foreword

Flight is an amazing privilege.

To view the world from the heavens and the wondrous sights the sky offers is one of life's true gifts. And it is one that I have been so very fortunate to enjoy for my three decades aloft.

Through flight I have travelled the world and witnessed the most incredible sights, both at sea-level and in the stratosphere. I have met all manner of wonderful people, from the keen young student pilots to the aged veterans of war with eyes and minds as sharp as they ever were. I have slept in a penthouse on the 60th floor as Hong Kong buzzed incessantly, and slumbered beneath the Cessna's wing when the only buzz was that of the cicadas. I have laughed until I cried and silently buried too many fellow pilots.

Through the stories within these pages I have chosen to share the wonders I have seen, felt and known. This book is not merely about aeroplanes, although they often provide the backdrop. This is about the unique people and places that aviation allows us to encounter. Therein we can find the real magic. Therein we can find 50 Tales of Flight.

Owen Zupp

***

The Author

Owen Zupp is an award-winning writer, published author and commercial pilot with nearly 19,000 hours of flight time. He has flown all manner of machines from antique biplanes to globe-trotting Boeings and shared the journey with readers around the world in a variety of publications.

The son of a decorated fighter pilot, Owen was born into aviation. His flying career has taken him from outback Australia to the rugged mountain ranges of New Guinea, the idyllic islands of Micronesia and across the oceans of the world to the United States, Europe, Africa and beyond.

Whether witnessing rocket launches from 40,000 feet or circumnavigating Australia for charity in a tiny two-seat training aircraft, Owen has cherished every minute aloft. Flight is not merely his profession, it is his passion.

For my little co-pilots.

Ruby, Hannah, Elizabeth and Hayden.

***

50 Tales of Flight

1

Golden Days

Thumbing through a folder some years back in another futile attempt to organise my filing cabinet, I came across a carefully stored certificate. It had not seen the light of day for some time, but it was instantly recognisable by the wings that adorned its upper edge as my 'First Solo Certificate'. With a rope-like border and an instructor's signature penned across its face, one particular feature leapt out at me; the date. Whilst the day and month were just around the corner, the year was another matter. After some quick arithmetic, the significance of the date became more substantial, it was nearly twenty five years since I had gone 'solo'.

Could that be right? A quarter of a century? I pondered the concept for a moment. Twenty five years can mean many things to many people. It can be a landmark of marriage for a happy couple or an inconceivable eon to a school student in their final year. As a parent, it's a blink. To a pilot it can be just another coincidence of numbers, volumes of which have already been carefully inked into a series of treasured log books.

For some reason this alignment of the calendar had struck a sentimental chord in me. Certificate in hand, I sat at my desk and reflected on where the time might have gone. It wasn't long before the blanks were filled in with a sea of memories and the trace of a grin gathered at the corner of my mouth.

In my mind's eye I can still see the ground at Camden Airport falling away from as the Cessna 152 leapt into the air, unburdened by my absent mentor in the right hand seat. Climbing away from runway 06, I was squinting into the morning sun as 17 year-olds didn't generally wear sunglasses back then. Wheeling 'Mike Alpha Whisky' onto the downwind leg and having time to realise that I was all alone. And loving it. With the checks complete, the base turn came too soon and it was time to ready the aeroplane for the approach. Managing the intricacies of speed, flap, power and trim, I rolled onto final to be greeted by the welcoming runway. The clearance to land crackled through the overhead speaker and I reached down to quickly acknowledge with the hand microphone. (Headsets were for airline pilots!) Down to earth again, but my life was changed forever. As a schoolboy, excitement overwhelmed any sense of significance.

Since that clear and calm summer morning, I have been very fortunate to fly a variety of machines and meet an even wider array of interesting people, some of whom have unfortunately not survived the aviator's journey. Flight offers so much to we mere mortals, from simple pleasures to immense exhilaration and the darkest nights to the most remarkable dawns. Sometimes we take it for granted as complacency walks hand in hand with the human condition.

For my part, I was always going to fly. My Dad had flown all manner of aircraft from Mustangs and Meteors to Cessnas and Super Connies.

He'd flown in combat over 200 times and later in life spent numerous midnight hours relaying the sick and injured in the NSW Air Ambulance 'Queen Airs'. The warbling of 'out of synch' propellers overhead was our signal that Dad would be home soon. As a kid, I would loiter around airports at every opportunity, scrounging rides where possible. There was no barbed wire or security fence to stop curious kids like me clambering up onto wing roots and gawking at cockpits through cupped hands. We were hangar rats and the hangars were full of cheese. Back at home, I would perch on our garage roof with binoculars and scan above for all and sundry as they criss-crossed the sky.

When it came my turn to learn to fly, I found a job as a paramedic that paid relatively well and afforded me enough time off to fly and study. At the time it felt like the Department of Health should simply directly credit my pay to the flying school accounts. Believe it or not, $47/hour private hire for a Tomahawk was quite an amount. With Dad as my instructor, my first school was the now-defunct Sydney Airways before moving to the now-defunct Royal Aero Club of NSW. Early starts and frost-covered windscreens were preceded by briefings in our garage at home. My working week revolved around my flying and when navigation exercises came into play, the anticipation was almost unbearable. Mum would pack us up with sandwiches and a Thermos of tea and we would venture to exotic locations like Coolah, Taree or Tamworth, navigating by charts that back then didn't cost a cent and landing without incurring an invoice. As I shared my sandwich and Dad his wisdom, I didn't realise how golden these days were. He would die of cancer within five years.

To be paid to fly was unfathomable, yet that's just what the Royal

Aero Club did for me as a lowly Grade 3 Instructor. Pulling out six Piper Tomahawks in early morning darkness and fuelling them one by one was a small price to pay to be allowed to fly for a living. Paid a salary and flying around ninety hours a month of single-hour lessons, my fellow instructor, Roland Parker, and I thought we'd died and gone to heaven. To simply get a slot in the training circuit, you'd await the control tower's call to the office to tell you when to start up and taxi, before shutting down in the run-up bay and waiting again, this time for a 'green light' from the tower. Finally, you'd get in the air. To see the veritable ghost town that Bankstown has now become borders on heart-breaking. Today we drive around a cyclone-fenced perimeter and where a sea of aeroplanes once sat, now only grass grows. The social hub of the old Aero Club where engineers and pilots would gather has been demolished. These are indeed very different times.

From instructing at Bankstown I went wandering to the north-west, to the Kimberleys and the beautiful land that is the Australian outback. There were scenic flight swarms over the Bungle Bungles and lone charters to all corners of the Northern Territory and Western Australia. Pre-dawn pre-flights were performed to the amazing backdrop of vast electrical storms over the Timor Sea and torrential downpours that changed the face of the scenery from wasteland to waterfalls in minutes. Along with the other young pilots, we made mistakes and learnt valuable lessons each day before retiring to the Argyle Tavern; it was paradise.

The beautiful Australian outback is only one of nature's canvases that I've been privileged to experience. New Guinea's lush highlands and interesting airstrips, some still covered in World War II Pierced-Steel-

Planking made up only part of the challenge; the rapidly changing weather being the other. Drinking from coconuts and boiling rice and fresh eel on the water's edge near Balimo. Ferrying an Islander aircraft to the tiny island of Yap in Micronesia and passing the numerous shallow atolls, complete with wrecked and rusting vessels caught on their barbs. Clambering over bullet-riddled Japanese Zeros and ferreting out an inverted Grumman Hellcat, now overgrown by vines.

From the flight levels there has been the rugged, war-torn landscape of Afghanistan and the frozen earth around Stalingrad where farmers somehow eke out a harvest each year. At 60 degrees south, icebergs float by day and the Southern Lights dance by night like an electric green curtain. Descending over Europe at dawn to break clear over the Thames and the city of London cannot help but remind one of those brave crews who limped home along the same route over sixty years ago with no Flight Management System to guide them. The lava flows of the Hawaiian Islands glowing by night and the US west coast illuminated by the spectacular efflux of a rocket launched out of Vandenberg.

Excitedly watching the world rocket by on my first flight in a 737, or the world spin around through the bubble canopy of a Mustang. Thoughtfully waltzing my Tiger Moth around the Glasshouse Mountains on the way to Toowoomba, my Dad's hometown and final resting place. Flight can be as diverse as the scenery we gaze down upon and the people we meet.

There have been less than picturesque moments too; a magneto blowing off my Cessna 310 before diverting into Meekatharra, a cylinder-head separating on a Cessna 210 and limping home to

5

Kununurra, a forced landing near Kanangra Walls in the Blue Mountains and a free ride home in the Careflight helicopter. Watching the demise of institutions like the Royal Aero Club of NSW and Ansett Airlines, whose pilot's wings and memories I still treasure. These hurdles along the way were the pot-holes on what has predominantly been a great road and has added character to the journey. They are also reminders that the road should be driven with due respect. That degree of respect should always be the same, be it a Beechcraft or a Boeing. It's a small price to pay for such a great privilege.

Twenty five years may sound like an eon; but it's a snapshot. There is still so much to see and do and there is no vantage point superior to that of the cockpit. It is a viewpoint for all of us to cherish. In the years to come, it is a world I will share with my children, as my father did with me.

So how did I celebrate the anniversary? I went flying. Away from home, I dawdled into a flying school in Queensland and became the student once more. My competency on the Piper Tomahawk was checked out over the scenic Sunshine Coast and in the rather gusty circuit. The instructor beside me wasn't born when my aviation trek began at Camden, but his youth offered a sense of continuity to the whole process. It was all ahead of him still and I envied that a little. As he climbed out, locked the door and gave me the 'thumbs up', it was reminiscent of a scene I had been lucky enough to offer my students many times before.

Solo once again, I lapped the circuit and looked at the world with eyes of that eager 17 year-old, briefly pondering the 25 years still to come. The crackle of the headset, the straining windsock and the welcoming strip of asphalt blend into the challenge of landing that has not faded with time. A challenge that is always relished by those who fly.

The joy of flying has lost none of its charm for me. The sights, sounds and sense of freedom; it is hard imagining life without it. We who aviate are very fortunate and flight is something we should always share and treasure. It doesn't matter which aircraft, weather or setting, when the earth falls away from the wheels, life is good.

*****

2

Auld Lang Syne

Unbelievably, the year is now down to its final hours. It has passed by leaving my children a little older and me none the wiser it would seem. The skies have again been kind to me these past twelve months, so as the champagne pops and the fireworks illuminate Sydney Harbour, my thoughts will again drift to an aviator now passed, who set me on my journey amongst the clouds.

He was a quiet man, short in stature but with arms made strong by a youth of combat and cane-cutting. He was predominantly self-educated, for drought and the Great Depression had stolen much of his childhood and any chance of a formal education. As a commando in the jungles of New Guinea, his kit-bag had been crammed with books on aerodynamics and aircraft while his dreams were of a life free of the earth's muddy bonds. But it was merely a dream for a lad with a big heart and no apparent claim to the elevated world of aviation. At the war's end, he traded the humidity of the jungle for the nuclear devastation of Hiroshima before finally wending his way home to Australia after years away at war.

Out of uniform he found it hard to settle down, drifting from one sugar-cane field to another with a few belongings strapped to the rear of his motorcycle. It was hard, hot labour to bring the mighty cane down by hand with snakes underfoot and insects clinging to the raw nectar running down his bare back. At the end of the sugar season, ultimately the road once again led him to the military, but this time as a mechanic in the Royal Australian Air Force. Finally surrounded by the machines he loved, he flourished in the hands-on application of his newly discovered knowledge. With money in his pocket and a home on the air base, he would spend his free hours studying aviation and paying for private flying lessons at the civilian school just across the tarmac. His dream was coming true, although his stunted education continued to form a barrier to any career in the sky; until fate dealt its hand.

With the outbreak of the Korean War in 1950, the air force was now depleted in its supply of post-war pilots. It called for volunteers from amongst its ranks and when a kindly commanding officer countersigned the young mechanics application, his world was changed forever. Within 18 months he had transitioned from repairing airframes to flying fighter combat missions over North Korea. As a Sergeant Pilot he would fly over two hundred sorties at the helm of a Gloster Meteor in the lethal ground attack role which saw many of his squadron mates killed in action. On one occasion, his own canopy was blown off by enemy fire and shrapnel was embedded in his face. Even so, he limped the damage jet home and flew two missions the next day. He returned home a decorated veteran and finally completed his formal education at night school.

He married an air force corporal who he had met prior to leaving for

Korea when she had processed his departure paperwork. Together they moved from base to base before a civil career ultimately called. From international airlines to cloud-seeding, flight instruction to target-towing, there was very little that the' short boy from the Australian bush didn't fly at some stage in the next 40 years. Yet in the 23,000 hours aloft and countless aircraft types, training always held a special place for him. The chance to mentor the next generation of pilots was something he valued as he always recalled how close his dream had come to never eventuating. If he saw a desire to fly in a young set of eyes, he would go the extra mile to make it happen.

He saw that desire in me from a young age and set an example that I still aspire to achieve. As an instructor he was unsurpassed and held in the highest regard by his peers. He had the knack of explaining complex concepts in simple terms with a million 'rules of thumb' to match. For him flight was always magnificent, but never elite. He cringed at the brash, slicked-back, sunglasses brigade but had endless patience for the struggling student who was trying their very best. He had fought in the jungle and stared down the tracer bullets that struck his jet, yet he never swore in front of women and always stood when they entered the room; he was old school.

To me he passed down so much more than the manipulative skills needed to fly an aeroplane. He instilled airmanship, a sense of command and an ultimate respect for the aircraft and the environment in which it operates. He loathed complacency and arrogance and highlighted that disciplined flying presented the greatest challenge and the most satisfaction. He set the bar very high and I was privileged to have such an outstanding mentor.

So as another year draws to a close, spare a thought for that special person who inspired you or guided you in your fledgling hours aloft. Revisit their lessons and strengths and give thanks for their patience and knowledge. Recount some of their anecdotes and share them with friends and family this New Year's Eve. It is a real gift to take to the sky, but without a steady guiding hand along the way, the journey can be fraught with potential dangers and self-doubt.

If it's possible, make contact with your mentor and thank them for their effort. It will mean the world to them and offer a chance to share the hours that have been logged since you last spoke. I would dearly love to speak with the man from the bush who taught me all that I know today and hear more of his pearls of wisdom. However, for me that is no longer an option as cancer took him nearly twenty years ago when I was still a young bush pilot taking my own first steps. Even so, as I sit around this New Years Eve surrounded by family I will spare him a thought and a silent word of thanks. He was the best pilot I ever met. He was my Dad.

Flying Officer Phillip Zupp M.I.D. AM (US) 1925-1991

*****

3

Unforgiving

Over recent times tragic news seems to have become all too frequent for the aviation community. While on the other side of the Indian Ocean the loss of the two Albatross aircraft dealt a single massive blow, here in Australia a series of accidents in just a few days has further added to the count. The national broadcaster's senior helicopter pilot and crew were lost, just as the news of an ill-fated mercy flight filtered down the wire. Only hours later, a senior sports pilot and his passenger went missing with a fatal outcome. The terrible loss of life in New Zealand when a hot air balloon was destroyed and a Tiger Moth crash saw the passing of John Fisher; a man who had once flown his Tiger from the United Kingdom to raise funds for charity. In the cruellest manner, it seemed we were all reminded that tragedy is the ever-present companion in the skies we seek to transit.

As the son of a former combat fighter pilot, I had grown up around the potentially fatal nature of aviation. As I flicked enthusiastically through fading photographs of fast jets, my father would answer my questions in an even tone. Often my enquiries with reference to the pilots was met with, "He got killed by ground fire near Haeju", or "I think he put a Mirage in off the coast during a training exercise". Their young faces beneath flying helmets still stare back at me so many years later.

My own first encounter with the harsh lessons of aviation started as a student pilot. Still a paramedic by trade, I stood at the Royal Aero Club counter as the crash horn sounded and the ominous black, oily plume rose from beyond the runway's end. Off duty, I drove my car the short distance around the airfield perimeter and entered the factory where the Piper Cherokee Six had plunged vertically through the roof. One burnt survivor has been thrown onto the rooftop, while I dragged another from the smoke-filled building. Four remained in the wreck, still strapped into their seats; lifeless. Any complacency about aviation that youth may have been tempted to bestow upon me was banished at that very moment.

In the losses of recent times, as is so often the case, there are not necessarily any common themes. Each was in a different type of aircraft, with the weather varying from despicable to fine and clear. The pilots ranged vastly in experience and their operations covered the spectrum from private flying to commercial aviation. The only shared trait seemed to be the tragic outcome.

I read through the various news reports with a strong dose of suspicion, borne of decades reading of ill-informed, sensationalist reporting. Details seemed to change by the hour and rumours took on the status of fact until the next piece of hearsay could be generated in the public domain. What could not be disputed was the life-altering impact of these accidents upon so many. To such a backdrop, one by one I recalled the faces of those that I had seen lost at the brutal edge of aviation. As I penned each name, the sobering truth was rammed home to me; no one is immune.

The list of names was far longer than I had anticipated. They ranged from pilots with whom I had shared a meal and conversation, to close friends and work colleagues. Nearly all of them were commercial pilots eking out a living in general aviation, though some had also been lost pursuing their passion just for the love of it. Some were starting their journey, excited at their first gainful employment and some were experienced mentors in the service of the nation's aviation regulator.

One by one I recalled their faces. The 'old hand' Bill whose ultimate oversight in forty years of safe flying was not spotting the glider that sheared off his Bonanza's tailplane. And Brinley, celebrating at the local restaurant at the news he'd secured a position with the national carrier only to perish nights later, circling into a black hole in rural Australia in the foulest of weather. Trevor, whose single-engined fish spotting aircraft had force landed at dusk into the frigid waters, only to survive the impact, but not the swim to shore. 'Freddo', who'd tried one too many hair-raising flying feats at too low an altitude, only to pancake into the rising terrain. Alan and Peter, who had been searching for another aeroplane when their own Cessna's engine had failed over inhospitable terrain. Fernando, who descended gently into the ground in the wee hours with a full load in his Baron. My fellow freight pilots who had been lost within a couple of months in a bleak, wet winter of low cloud and icing levels. On and on the list continued as face after face stared back at me.

14

Admittedly, there were those who had been sticking their neck out further than the rules and common sense would advise. But for most it was simply a case of the odds stacking up against them in a series a compounding smaller events; the classic 'Swiss Cheese' model of Dr. James Reason. For a few it was the simple bad luck scenario of wrong place-wrong time. Universally, however, they are all still with me; even though I had not thought of many of them in recent years. They are with me every day. They are with me as I flight plan and as I retract the landing gear. They are with me as the day becomes night and as the weather turns dark and walls of water confront me. They are with me always.

They are not evil spectres awaiting my demise, they are those who have gone before and paid the ultimate price. They paid for their harsh lessons with their lives and I am now the benefactor of their loss. In many ways, I owe them for the joy I have experienced in the skies above. They may have gone before, but they have stayed behind to tell me when enough is enough and when danger is lurking. They are there when the hair stands up on the back of my neck. They level the playing field and stand on the kerb whenever the temptation to cut a corner may exist.

They were acquaintances, colleagues and close friends who lived and breathed for aviation. I count myself as fortunate to have thus far safely encountered my way, but this is not an automatic right. It requires an ongoing commitment to safety and discipline at all times and anything less is to dishonour those who have sacrificed so much. We call the skies our home and it is not a dangerous place to encounter. However, as those who have been lost recently and in the distant past can attest, aviation can be very unforgiving.

15

*****

4

Engine Failure!

As an Approved Test Officer, I enjoyed the task of testing candidates for the issue of a shiny new licence or rating. By and large, the students were well prepared, knowledgeable and as keen as mustard. On a June afternoon in 1993 I was tasked with a Commercial pre-licence test for an overseas candidate who was champing at the bit to return home and join his national airline. Clear skies, an aeroplane fresh from its 100 hourly servicing and a diligent student set the tone for a pleasurable flight; well, for the first couple of hours anyway.....................

Azlan possessed a very quiet manner that somewhat belied the fierce determination with which he approached his flying training. As he leaned over the wing of the Aerospatiale TB20 Trinidad and re-calculated his endurance and performance figures, he was a picture of concentration. To this point we had successfully navigated our way from Bankstown to Goulburn and northwest to our present port of call, Cowra. He had flown the aeroplane smoothly and countered the periodic 'examiner-induced challenges' that inherently crop up during a test flight. From here it was on to Mudgee, thence a return to Bankstown and hopefully a recommendation for the fully fledged licence test. His preparation and planning had been superb and his chosen routing reflected his comprehension of my perennial precursor; "bearing in mind that this is a single engined aeroplane". A philosophy highlighting that a few extra miles over friendly terrain can present a pilot with potential landing fields, recognisable landmarks and options should things go quiet up front.

With the paperwork completed and more than adequate fuel evenly distributed between the two wing tanks, we fired up and launched once more into the beautiful skies over western NSW. Once established in level flight, I adopted the role of 'employer' and advised Azlan that the 'passengers' at Mudgee had cancelled their flight and he was now to return to Bankstown directly, "bearing in mind that this is a single engined aeroplane". With the highway to Katoomba a short way ahead and the security of a navigational beacon and an airstrip at the Blue Mountains township, a little planning would result in a fairly straightforward trip home. In the only tarnished point of the flight, Azlan estimated a heading and wheeled the aircraft eastward to point in the general direction of Bankstown. The proposed route was relatively void of features and characterised by the mountainous 'tiger country' of the Great Dividing Range. Whilst seemingly a poor option, he was not breaking any rules and was acting 'In Command Under Supervision'. At worst it was a questionable technique and warranted mention after the flight, but after all that is what training is about.

As we skirted to the south of Oberon, Azlan came up for air, refined his heading and made good a direct track to Bankstown Airport.

Whilst clipping along at 1,500 feet above the ground, I felt a little uneasy, though not unduly so. Despite rumours to the contrary, the engines of light aircraft do not immediately enter 'auto-rough' at night, over rugged terrain or on Trans-Pacific ferry flights. Whilst not perhaps prudent, our track was perfectly legitimate.

I was midway through convincing myself of this fact when a flickering of light caught my eye. The Trinidad's digital fuel flow gauge was hopping around without rhyme or reason, whilst the engine continued to purr and the good old fashioned analogue fuel flow needle sat steady like the Rock of Gibraltar. New fangled gadgetry, maybe, but either way it prompted me to look outside for a potential forced landing field; just in case. As luck would have it, a lone small clearing was just off the right and I asked Azlan to enter a gentle turn toward it. He had still not noticed the 'Digi-Flow' jumping around when I drew it to his attention and started to talk him through the trouble-shooting process. When the analogue needle started to reflect the readings of its digital counterpart my interest heightened and we completed further checks without delay. The engine now began to surge in company with the cockpit indications so at this point I took over and called up Sydney Flight Service to put them in the loop. I had gone from 'fat, dumb and happy' to 'rather concerned' in the grand total of about ninety seconds.

Our lone paddock approached beneath and the engine surges were becoming so significant that maintaining our height was becoming an increasingly difficult task. I advised Flight Service that we were 55 miles and bearing 255 degrees from Sydney whilst I still had the chance, as VHF radio had been 'in and out' at this low altitude. I was contemplating a precautionary landing with the sporadic power that

19

remained when a total engine failure took me out of the decision making process. I trimmed the aircraft for the glide and knowing VHF communication was at a premium, I alerted Sydney of our worsening predicament and manually switched on the Emergency Locator Transmitter (ELT). Again through the emergency checks and still no luck. Fortunately I had already decided upon the field and a course of action, though it was becoming increasingly apparent that it was going to be very tight and far from a smooth ride. I told Azlan to secure everything in the cockpit and that when we were on the ground, he was to exit and get clear of the aircraft without delay.

Assured of making the field, I started lowering the flaps and landing gear before advising Flight Service that I would shortly be going 'off-the-air'. I then dispensed with my electrics in an attempt to minimise the chance of a post-impact fire. The world was getting very big in the window as I aligned myself with the paddock ahead and I decided that it was way too short to make it over the trees on the approach and still pull up by the far end. As I had done at airstrips in the outback and New Guinea, I slipped the aircraft down between the trees at the near end in an effort to maximise the amount of cleared ground to land on. The foliage rushed by, there was a short squeak of the stall warning horn and then the wheels hit. Thump!

70 knots or so across an unprepared surface is a wild ride. I was standing on the brakes, keeping straight and hoping for the best when a sizeable rock jutted up ahead. Unable to swerve to any great degree, I braced thinking this was going to hurt. I tensed my guts and for a nanosecond thought of the control column spearing into me. Bang! The right gear struck the rock and we were OK; still hurtling across the paddock, but OK. With not enough room for my liking, I heaved

back on the stick and kicked in my left boot, effectively 'ground-looping' a nosewheel aeroplane. The right landing gear seemed to give at this point and we slewed sidewards, shuddering to a halt just short of the trees. I swung around to tell Azlan to get out. With the disturbed dust still suspended in the late afternoon air I was looking at an empty seat, an open gull wing door and the northbound end of a southbound student. That lad sure knew how to follow instructions!

I soon followed my breathless student and having taken a moment, returned to a rather forlorn aeroplane. Paranoia forced me to inspect the Trinidad's tanks which revealed a copious amount of fuel in both wings: Phew! I tried calling up on the radio and thankfully established contact with an approaching aircraft that had already been diverted to the area. I advised the pilot that we were all OK and he relayed to Flight Service our exact position and further information. (He had one of those new fangled GPS things.) It was getting dark and with the temperature dropping, we threw on our jackets and gathered firewood in case we were there for the night. Fortunately, the Careflight helicopter was on the job from Westmead Hospital and making a bee-line through the night sky to our position. Once in range, I spoke to the pilot and described the field, potential hazards and where the aircraft lay in the paddock. (In my previous life as a paramedic, establishing a landing field had been part of the training.) Within minutes I heard the thumping rotors and spotted the chopper's lights to which I replied with every light, strobe and beacon the little Trinidad possessed. The helicopter's spotlight turned night into day as it manoeuvred with due caution and touched down a short distance away. I returned my Trinidad to a dark, lifeless state before we were both guided by the crewman to the helicopter and our ride back home. Strapped in, the rotors spun up and we rose into absolute darkness, steadily accelerating into the void. Slowly the glow of Sydney's lights became a visible horizon and I knew we were on our way. It was only then that I think I stopped to draw a breath.

Twenty years have passed since we came to ground just shy of Kanangra Walls and there was definitely a lot that I gleaned from the experience that has hopefully held me in good stead ever since. First and foremost, my general philosophy of flight planning in single engined aircraft was upgraded to a strict personal doctrine. Whilst recognising that it is not *always* possible, the trade off of distance must be made whenever friendly terrain is on offer. Be aware of terrain, lowest safe altitudes, airfields and navaids in the planning phase when you have the time available for consideration. Even when venturing into instrument flying and multi-engine aeroplanes, icing conditions and single-engine ceilings still call for a healthy respect of the surrounding terrain.

I have always had one eye out the window for a field when I've been flying single-engined aeroplanes. For the thousands of hours looking, it probably has only made real a difference for me on this one occasion, but it was a life full of difference. By being aware of my only option, deciding to turn towards it and formulating a potential plan *before* things turned ugly, probably saved my neck. Utilise the available time to an absolute maximum as in a gliding aeroplane time is measured in seconds and equates to the haemorrhaging of valuable altitude. My actions weren't the hallmark of exceptional skill; they were simply the application of the training we all receive as licensed pilots.

Another reason that we walked away that day was that I was current on practice forced landings and I had a fair amount of experience on short runways that were void of asphalt and touch-down markers. My currency at the time was due to my job as an instructor, but ever since I have insisted on a dual check in my private flying to ensure that I'm still up to speed on unexpected occurrences such as engine failures and go-arounds. In addition, bush flying gave me an appreciation of speed control and the feel of an aeroplane at that slower, sluggish end of the performance envelope. It gave me a greater sense and appreciation of the approaching stall than is necessarily offered by the warning devices fitted to aircraft. Again, it was an issue of currency. Even if your flying is always out of long, sealed runways it is good form to integrate some short field arrivals and departures into your comings and goings. You never know when you may need to call upon these skills in anger.

Personally, I lost a degree of innocence in the Blue Mountains that afternoon. I had always looked upon *every* patch of urban clearing as a potential forced landing field, which in retrospect was a little naïve and over-confident. These days I'm more selective. Ironically, my first flight back after the forced landing was a couple of days later in the form of a single-engine night test; talk about getting back in the saddle! I can now confess to sweaty palms a couple of times that night and I almost became a believer in the auto-rough setting. Notwithstanding, I have continued to fly, own and enjoy single engine aeroplanes ever since. The experience in no way deterred me from 'singles', it merely reinforced my belief in how they should be operated.

Statistically, engine failures are not a common occurrence. That does not relieve us as pilots of the obligation to be prepared for the loss of engine power. It is an obligation to ourselves, our passengers and those who dwell beneath the sky we transit. As in all aspects of aviation, sound knowledge and preparation can give a pilot a distinct advantage. That advantage can in turn be pressed home, with the maintenance of skills and a common sense approach to all aspects of the operation. Aviation is about setting and meeting our own standards, not merely those imposed by instructors, examiners and flight-test forms. Ideally, for every flight, we should always be "prepared, knowledgeable and as keen as mustard".

*****

5

Flight of a Lifetime

To fly around Australia was not an idea that happened upon me overnight. It was an idea hatched in childhood, and ultimately flown solo decades later. Eight months in planning and eighteen days in execution, I suspect the planning would have been somewhat quicker if it had not grown into such a public exercise with such a genuine, interested following.

The Australian centenary of flight was an appropriate milestone to commemorate, but it also provided an excellent base-line to highlight just how far aviation had come in one hundred years. True, I covered around 13,000 kilometres across both remote and overwater segments, but the task was nothing beyond the level of an appropriately licensed and experienced private pilot. With all of the modern infrastructure, technology and support at our fingertips, what would have been a major undertaking even fifty years ago, is now relatively straightforward.

With planning complete and the all-Australian Jabiru J230D aircraft assembled and decked out in her 'There and Back' scheme, the planets aligned to promise an on-schedule departure on May 5th. In the days preceding, there were numerous media commitments to attend to, but more importantly, technical matters to become familiar with; from spark plugs to changing a wheel. There is no substitute for 'hands on' time with your aeroplane and fortunately, I was never called upon to repeat the tasks in the field as the Jabiru happily hummed its way around the country.

The day before departure saw low, grey and wet skies over Bundaberg. However, the synoptic weather chart suggested that the trough may move out to sea and a big, happy high pressure system would dominate at least the first few days of my flight. The chart was right and May 5th dawned without a cloud in the sky and my departure from Bert Hinkler's home-town was set for 10am.

After a few final formalities, I departed Bundaberg right on time and watched the country town fall away to my left as I initially set course to dawdle along the picturesque coastline. It was only when the aircraft was established in level flight and the 'housekeeping' had been attended to, that I actually realised that the 'There and Back' journey was finally underway. It was a great sense of elation with a twinge of 'Wow, it's a long way to go!', when I thought of my wife and kids. Yet as I scanned the crystal skies above, I just knew that this would be a flight to remember.

The route was loosely based upon points of Australian aviation significance; from Longreach, the home of QANTAS to Minlaton, home to the oft overlooked pioneer, Harry Butler. Yet there were places of personal significance too. From Kununurra and the Kimberleys, where I had flown as a young charter pilot to

Toowoomba where my father was laid to rest twenty years ago. The selection of these waypoints made each leg interesting and offered a carrot at the end of each day's flying. Rather than being merely a long distance flight, it was more akin to unravelling a scroll, with each new page introducing fascinating words, images and people.

In fact, it was in this way that the flight most readily exceeded expectations. After such thorough planning, there were very few surprises in terms of aircraft performance, airspace or procedures. However, no matter how imaginative I may have been, I could never have grasped the intangible beauty of the land and the warmth of people that I encountered. For this reason alone, I would encourage pilots, one and all, to set course far beyond their regular boundaries at least once.

Over the course of such a flight, it is the diversity of the scenery that can leave an overwhelming impression. That is not to say that there are not individual sights that take the breath away. The majestic Lake Argyle in the Kimberley region or the serene endlessness of the Nullarbor Plain are both very moving in their own special way. However, when you can depart the coastal port of Broome over pristine aqua waters and track along pure white beaches before striking the rustic reds of the Pilbara within an hour, it is nothing short of inspiring. This diversity of colour, wildlife and inhabitation essentially captures both ends of the Australian scenic spectrum.

To take in such a view from between 500 and 5,000 feet, enables one to really embrace the richness of the terrain. The land below has real detail and the passage of the shadows as the day develops provides yet another perspective on the rich canvas below. There are long abandoned ruins of long forgotten towns and flocks of birds that give the impression of a vast blanket skimming from paddock to paddock.

Even the so-called 'remote' regions stimulate the senses with their jagged, jutting ridges and gun-barrel roads between distant settlements. And within these towns are people so unaffected by the frantic pace of urban reality. Calm and content, inhabiting settlements that have changed little over recent times, yet generous beyond compare. At Murchison Station near Kalbarri in Western Australia I had one such experience.

Over 150 years old, the station had once played host to the famed aviator Sir Charles Kingsford Smith, while I spent the night in shearing sheds of convict vintage. It was a small room with a tiny single window and locks on the outside of the door to contain the convicts who had constructed the dwelling. Nearby, two fallen aviators from 90 years ago are buried and the experience of visiting their graves will not soon be forgotten. My hosts were more like old friends, free of false pretension but long on sincerity and warmth. Their manner reflected the very honest nature of the land on which they dwell.

Yet beyond the beauty, I always maintained the aviator's sense of respect. The terrain below can at any time become a landing field for the pilot of a single-engined aeroplane. To this end, the land and the nearest water were endlessly assessed in case the untoward occur. Conversely, flying over Bass Strait or the Spencer Gulf, I was continually aware of the distance to my next landfall.

As part of my preparation, the Jabiru was stocked with supplies to cater for these contingencies. From emergency rations and fresh water, to space blankets, waterproof matches and life jackets. Survival gear was packed for minimum weight, but maximum effect. Certain essential items were also very close at hand in a bright red 'grab bag' should egress from the aircraft be particularly rapid for some reason. Furthermore, the aircraft was equipped with a satellite tracking system with an alert mode, dual VHF radios, transponder and an emergency beacon. In conjunction with the submission of detailed flight plans, I was always confident that I would not perish under the wing like so many pioneer aviators had done decades before. And yet, it is sound airmanship to cater for the worst and be thankful for the best.

The weather was one variable beyond my control and planning, other than the month of May historically providing fine weather and favourable winds. However, in this area I was absolutely blessed. The high pressure system loitered over the inland for so long, I thought it had been tethered there and not only provided fair weather, but tailwinds across the Top End of the country. From the flight's mid-point at Perth in Western Australia, I always seemed to be a couple of days ahead of troughs, fronts and poor weather.

There was a little weather to dodge over the stretch of water between the mainland and Tasmania, but nothing significant. Low cloud near the nation's capital, Canberra, and storms near Gunnedah provided the only real hindrance, but otherwise it was stress-free visual flying. I'd like to take credit for those clear, blue skies, but that area is well beyond my expertise.

The other variable that lay beyond my scope of influence was aircraft reliability. Like the weather, the Jabiru J230 did not miss a beat and performed at better than book figures for the entire trip. Sipping around 23 litres per hour to achieve nearly two miles per minute, the

Jabiru made an efficient vehicle in which to circumnavigate the nation. Its high wing both afforded shade and an ideal view of the grand display below. With two seats, the space to the rear provided ample room for all of my equipment and never presented a weight issue that allowed for anything less than full tanks for every departure. It was like a well finished utility vehicle that never had to deal with the bumps in the road when venturing cross country.

Aside from an oil change, filters and the tyre pressures being topped up in Perth, there was no need for additional maintenance for the entire flight. Each day I would remove the cowls for a closer look and each day I found an incredibly clean engine ready for another days work. From icy frosts to sweltering heat, the little machine kept on performing and I played my part by always treating the aircraft and its engine with due respect.

When Runway 14 loomed large in the windscreen at Bundaberg for the final landing, I reminded myself that the flight wasn't over yet. However, when the aircraft was parked and the propeller stopped, I allowed myself a sigh of mixed relief and reflection. Beyond that there were family and friends there to greet me and media to speak with. A reception was held at the Hinkler Hall of Aviation and in the shadow of my hero's memorabilia I enjoyed a wonderful afternoon of catching up with one and all. Along the way the flight had reached its target of $10,000 for the Royal Flying Doctor Service and for me that was a personal goal that meant so much.

Once the dust had settled and I had retired to a house on the coast with my family, I had the first real chance to absorb what had transpired over the preceding weeks. I seemed to have endless tales and humorous anecdotes of the people and places I had encountered.

My family listened intently and ultimately they drew the same conclusions as the media and enquired, "Where are you off to next?" With all honesty, I replied that I really couldn't say, although I would dearly enjoy stretching the borders once again.

The freedom of flight is something that is so accessible to us in this modern day. To take the road less travelled amongst the cumulus and share the experience with those along the way is something I cannot recommend highly enough. It is an experience that I would dearly love to pursue again. Yet, whatever future flights and adventures may rise above the horizon and wherever those journeys may subsequently take me, I will never forget the month of May when I decided to simply fly 'There and Back'.

*****

In the Jabiru on my way around Australia. (Image: Australian Aviation)

The Boeing 737-800 at Dusk.

6

Behind Closed Doors

Hangar doors can be huge; as large as a football field in some cases. And behind those doors can exist a wonderland of surprises for those with a passion for all things that fly.

As a boy I remember peering through the gaps between hangar doors and trying to make out aerodynamic forms in the half-light. Perhaps identifying a shapely fin, or a registration mark emblazoned on the flanks. I would scout behind the doors of other hangars for there lay treasure of the schoolboy kind. Tucked away were broken up plywood aircraft crates that had now served their purpose, only to be reborn as cubby houses and billy carts.

To loiter around an airfield unchallenged by security patrols may be a thing of the past, but in its day it was a simple pleasure. Occasionally, those hangar doors were more than cracked and engineers and owners welcomed the curious kid with the wing-nut ears and freckled cheeks. Lifting me into the doorway of a war weary Douglas C-47, I was free to sit and 'biscuit-bomb' to my heart's content. And then there was old Syd Marshall's hangar that would make me drool with its Mustangs and Messerschmitts. Hanging from the roof, pushed into corners and anywhere they would fit were classic aircraft of a bygone era.

As my Dad and Syd would chat, I would climb into one of the Mustangs and dog-fight an unseen enemy with all of the sweat, but none of the danger, of aerial combat. I would check my six and heave the stick into my guts, pressing my chin to my chest and imagine the world fading to grey as the blood ran from my head....just as Dad told me it would. I would stare at the dials and comprehend the purpose of a few before Dad would climb onto the wing, strap me in and utter words like "friction" and "boost". I nodded knowingly with my most attentive of expressions which generally brought a broad grin from his face as he saw through my charade. "Carry On!" he would instruct before returning to Syd and proudly gesturing in my direction.

As I grew and took to the skies in my own right, the hangars now housed my precious places of work. On cold mornings I would drag the little Pipers, one by one, to the bowser and then the flight-line and at the day's end I would put them to bed. It was a task that I loved, particularly in the quiet times when everyone else had gone home. I still enjoyed making out the silhouettes in the half-light and listening to the creaking of the roof above me and the rattle of the doors behind me. It never ceased to amaze me how free the hangar doors were to rattle, but how darn stubborn they were when it came to pushing them open and closed.

The hangars still held their treasures too. At country airfields I would catch a glimpse of a Stearman or Tiger Moth through the cracks in the door. I once even saw row after row of Vampire jet 'tail booms' leaning against the wall while their shadowy pod-like cockpits sat on the dirt floor. I hurriedly scribbled down their markings on my flight plan to check against the entries in my Dad's log books at a later time.

Sometimes there were sad moments too. Once, the wreck of a Cessna was placed in the concealed corner of a hangar where I was employed. There had been fatalities including two chaps I had known. On one of those quiet evenings as I secured the hangar at the day's end, I wandered over and pondered at the wreckage. Surprisingly intact, the tell-tale creases gave away the fact that the fuselage had compressed with brutal force on impact before expanding once again. Signs of their suffering were still present in the cockpit and I couldn't help but think of their faces as I last remembered them. I don't know how long I stood there that evening; time seemed to stop. But I remember that it was dark and cold as I fumbled for the key to lock the hangar and walk to my car.

With the airlines came bigger aeroplanes and bigger hangars, but also bigger security cards. My days of loitering aimlessly had been replaced by check-points, hi-Viz vests and hearing protection. I was still in wonder of the machines, but some of their personality seemed to have left their form and had been replaced by a colder efficiency. Even so, this age of jets ultimately led me to their birthplace in Seattle where the hangars seem so large that they could generate their own weather systems. End on end, fuselage after fuselage of mighty Boeings are assembled before rolling out and making their way into the stratosphere. The enormous scale of the operation and the aircraft is breathtaking and a far cry from the discarded plywood sheets in the hangars of my childhood.

True, they may rattle in the wind, creak in the sun and provide a deafening orchestra in the rain, but at day's end they are still there with their precious steeds safe inside. Like the aeroplanes they house, hangars are merely metal and mouldings in their most basic sense. These hangars have stood strong as economies have cycled through boom and bust and they have farewelled failed companies and welcomed new hope. And if the walls could speak they could tell tales that would captivate the most critical listener with stories of far flung destinations, fledgling airlines and pilots and 'planes that never came home. They have borne silent witness to aviation's endless 'comings and goings' and yet there's probably even one or two that still recall that curious kid, the one with the wing-nut ears and the freckled cheeks.

*****

7

Decisions, Decisions

They say that our life is the sum of all of our decisions. Like some sort of organic flow chart that forks with 'yes, no and maybe' to lead us down a new and unknown path. At times, flying can almost fall into the same category, with an equal number of frustrating choices and loathsome grey areas. This week another aircraft was lost, caught up in the midst of descending weather and rising terrain. On hearing the news, I went through the frustrating round-about of 'if only' and wondered at what point there was no way out and at what point the pilot realised this.

Life's choices are also similar to aeronautical decisions in that our own experience can be a major factor. As an adolescent, we all tend to be a little more impetuous and impatient, with no real experience to use as a slide rule by which to gauge our actions. At that age there is very little ability to project forward and see how this might play out, we are far more 'in the moment'. At the controls of an aeroplane, an inexperienced pilot can be similarly affected. Without a sound appreciation of their own boundaries and little exposure to the proven limitations of those that have gone before, decisions may lack the 'fear factor' of an older hand. That healthy feeling of hair standing up on the back of the neck that says. "I've been here before" or "I've read about this". These mental checks are often the first 'red flag' that the present situation is starting to erode.

As a flight instructor, I have always been aware that teaching the manipulative skills of flying is the relatively easy part. Instilling airmanship, discipline and prudence is far more difficult. That involves influencing the perspective and behaviour of another, and that is never an easy task. Older students sometimes struggled with the 'pushing and pulling' of the aeroplane, but with life experience they generally grasped the mind-set easily. Younger students, even those with great skills, sometimes found mortality as a consequence of their actions to be an abstract concept. However, age and experience could not be seen solely as the defining factors either.

That demon 'complacency' can creep into the mind of the most capable aviators. Some years ago, a good friend of mine perished attempting a low-level manoeuvre with insufficient altitude or energy. He was a good pilot and a great guy, but his comfort zone had undoubtedly encroached upon his common sense on this occasion. A decision made on an impulse, on the spur of the moment, can have ramifications that last a lifetime for so many people.

It can be tempting to make decisions and pass judgement in retrospect, but this is also unhealthy. For the moment that we shake our head and assert that we could never make the same mistake, we have cracked the door for complacency to creep in. We have immediately asserted that we are 'better' than the pilot in question and 'above' such folly. It is far wiser to lament the loss and remind ourselves that we are all human. For whatever reason, the situation has conspired to bring down another aviator and we should respect their loss and remind ourselves of our own shortcomings.

So what's the answer? Well, there's no 'magic fix' as I see it. As long as there is a human, there is the vulnerability of the 'human factor'. Many of the accidents that come to mind have exceeded the limits of the airframe, the regulations or the constraints of the pilot's licence; so sticking to the rules is a good start. But it's only a start. There is legal and there is prudent, so to be relevant, we often have to factor our own comfort zone onto the limitations listed in the books. Five kilometres legal visibility may not be enough, even if you are able to appreciate what that visibility looks like in the real world.

An early decision is often a conservative decision. When deteriorating weather or shrinking fuel stocks start to cause concern, it is probably time to act. For the moment that concern enters the brain, it sucks up valuable mental processing capacity that is needed to make sound decisions. The further you fly down the funnel, the narrower your focus will become. Turning back, diverting, even out-landing in a paddock may be inconvenient, but YOU are still in control. Once you put the Weather Gods or gravity in the pilot's seat, you are entering very dangerous territory.

I have always believed that aviation is not inherently dangerous, but it can be incredibly unforgiving. For those that have danced with the devil and survived, the spectre of a hill in the clouds or a coughing engine has changed their outlook for the better for the rest of their days. However, their survival was more often through good luck than good judgement. It is a risky business to learn by taking the situation to the very edge of the envelope and that is best left to the trained hands of test pilots. We mere mortals are far better advised to play the safe hand and extricate ourselves before our apprehension becomes desperation. Take the early turn, the easy road and contemplate what may have been from the safety of an airfield.

Aviation is a skilled act undertaken in an unfamiliar environment. We are the guests of the Gods when we leave the earth. There are so many variables that may influence our journey along the way; the compressed time-frame of travelling at speed, the whimsical nature of the weather, the challenges of our own skill level, complacency and a need to get home. Like turning screws, their pressure grows with every minute that passes and every drop of fuel consumed. All the while, our mind is taxed and our human frailty is exposed.

It is a joy to fly in the skies above, but it is a privilege that is bound by our own human limitations. Our decisions mark the points at which we answer those challenges set before us and unfortunately those decisions can literally be a matter of life and death. Opt for an early decision, on the conservative side of the fence and live to fly another day. For those very decisions may lead to long-lasting outcomes for you and the ones you love. Fly safe my friends.

*****

8

History, Hamburgers and Horsepower

As settings go, the warbird enthusiast would be hard pressed to beat Chino Airport in southern California. Forty minutes from downtown Los Angeles and nestled amongst rural properties, the airport has a backdrop of snow-capped mountains which exist in perfect harmony with the warming influence of the Santa Anna breeze. An absolute setting of nature at its finest, yet at any given moment the peace can be shattered in the nicest possible way; by the awe-inspiring roar of an aircraft from a bygone era, refusing to go silently into history.

The time warp can begin from the minute you drive into Chino. Tucked between hangars and huts sits Flo's Diner, an absolute must for any visit to the airfield. Behind the old screen door waitresses hustle about with pots of coffee as jacketed pilots, engineers, and enthusiasts hunch over the nearby counter. The coffee is black, the eggs are over-easy and the menu keeps cardiologists in business. The walls are all but hidden by yellowing posters proclaiming support for 'Our Boys' at war and an array of photos portraying long gone men and machines. The background hum of conversation sits well with the bustle of laden trays and creates an atmosphere that has seemingly remained unchanged for over half a century. Flo's is more about character than cuisine.

It's best to breakfast at Flo's as lunch won't leave you with adequate time to dawdle through the two major museums at Chino; 'Planes of Fame' and 'Yanks'. The former is synonymous with the airfield, whilst Yanks is a relative newcomer, though no less impressive. Both are a treasure trove of aircraft that date back to before World War One, though the roaring piston engined aircraft of the second major conflict definitely make up the bulk of the collections. In company with the early jet fighters, the aircraft are not simply museum pieces and there are many living, breathing and flying examples that cast off the shelter of hangarage and show their wares at a variety of air shows throughout the year. For the fiscally advantaged, there is even the opportunity to back-seat in a P-40 Kittyhawk, or some similar machine. There is so very much on offer.

The long established, "Planes of Fame" museum welcomes you with a four-engined Flying Fortress on the front lawn. Aircraft from the earliest days of military aviation through to a specifically designated "Jet Hangar", feature static and flying examples of a vast range. Many of the flying examples have made the trek to the bright lights of nearby Hollywood and starred in such films as Pearl Harbour. Conveniently, the tremendous collection of Japanese aircraft allowed the "Planes of Fame" to participate in both sides of the battle. One such example, the Mitsubishi Zero, transcended the celluloid in times past and flew in actual combat over such Pacific islands as Iwo Jima and Tinian.

Wandering amongst the maze of hangars, all manner of aircraft can be encountered. They are from all continents and each come with their own history. French Ace Charles Nungesser's WWI biplane, a Canadian Spitfire from D-Day or an F-86 Sabre from Korea. The list is all but endless. A particularly attractive display sees the US Navy carrier-based contingent hangared in a style reminiscent of the USS Enterprise. Wings folded and crammed in, the sense of an aircraft carrier is tangible. Complete with side railings, semaphore flags and a shiny deck, the portholes are filled with a treasure chest of nautical memorabilia. It's a time warp within a time warp.

Like Santa's workshop with rivet-guns, a number of the hangars are dedicated to renewing or extending the life of these fine machines. Jigs, paint-shops and engine-trestles fill every corner to restore these stallions above and beyond their former glory. In one such hangar sits a forerunner of modern day 'stealth' technology. The Northrop N-9M is one of a kind, an original flying wing that harks back to the 1940s. Designed as a 1/3 scale flying example of a larger bomber, the N-9M was piloted by a lone pilot and used to prove a unique aerodynamic theory. Whilst its larger brethren did eventuate, it failed to go into major production and it would be decades before the concept was successful in the modern generation of stealth warriors. The museum's flying wing still takes to the sky and is another example of living history, rather than the dusty cabinets that characterise some collections.

Rare types are not the only medium by which history remains tangible. Seminars are monthly, 'joy flights' are on demand and air displays are definitely not to be missed. The 'member flights' in these historic warbirds are the ride of a lifetime. Strapped into one of these classics, you'll experience the real seat-squashing inertia of a high performance take-off, zoom climbs, tumbling rolls and high speed passes, all to the beautiful backdrop of pastures and raking ridge lines.

When you've finished crawling over the static display, prying into the workshop and cutting up the sky in a P-40 Kittyhawk, you'll need to make your way to the Yanks Museum at the other end of the airfield. 'Yanks' came about when Charles and Judith Nichols purchased their first aircraft in 1973 and in doing so planted the seed for what stands today as one of the world's largest private aircraft collections. The establishment of Yanks Air Museum at Chino subsequently came about in the 80s and has a focus on the preservation of American aviation history and technology. Totalling in excess of one hundred and fifty machines, and growing, it is phenomenal that all are original airframes that belong to the Museum. No replicas, no reproductions and no 'loaners'.

Entering the main hangar, one is immediately struck by the vast array of pristine, airworthy aircraft in an immaculate facility. An American flag stands near a pair of Curtiss JN-4D's, or 'Jennies', and seemingly announces the arrival of US military aviation. They are kept company by an immaculate selection of civil aeroplanes from the 'golden age' of aviation. A time in which the likes of Lindbergh crossed the Atlantic, though not before living through the perils of delivering the US Mail with the likes of Elrey Jeppesen. The B-1 Brougham afforded the pilot the luxury of forward visibility with a windscreen, something Lindbergh did without!

Striking in terms of position, stature and its brilliant yellow paint scheme stands a Naval Air Factory (NAF) N3N-3 Floatplane. This 'Stearman on floats' is perched high and represents a very small group of survivors. This example was void of a centre float until one surfaced inland at a Sacramento trailer park. Living its retirement out as a garden bed, the Museum acquired the sought after component and supplied the owner with a replacement planter. The old naval trainer is shadowed by a variety of warbird heavy metal. A surviving Douglas SBD-4 is fittingly in company with a 'bullet-holed' wing recovered from Guadalcanal. This 'Dauntless' is a true veteran having seen action in the Marianas Straits and the Truk and Marshall Islands. In contrast, the dive bomber's final posting was somewhat less lethal as it was used as a wind machine at MGM studios before being acquired in 1984. A Hollywood role that was filled by another of the collection's combat veterans, a Grumman TBF-1 Avenger.

The adjacent hangar houses a memorabilia display and restoration facility. Recognising the interest in this fascinating aspect of preserving history, the people at 'Yanks' have wisely included a walk-through the section where these fine machines are reborn. The line up is seemingly endless and each has a unique tale to tell. Perhaps most fascinating is the Model 11 "Ohka". Designed and utilised as a manned kamikaze craft, it was launched from the belly of a mother ship. A lethal dart, it glided at speeds of 630 km/h with a 1200kg warhead on board. Six examples were recovered post war and the ravages of time had taken its toll on the wooden flying surfaces of Yanks' model. In keeping with their policy, they sought to restore the Ohka to airworthy condition, though there is no intention of flying the aircraft. (After all, it was never designed with a system to land again.) This restoration goal created somewhat of a dilemma as the rather unique woodworking skills had not been used for many years. Unbelievably, the museum's Master Woodworker, Tony Furukawa, had learnt the needed techniques when he was apprenticed in 1944 to Mr. Kenichi Maeda. The Ohka's original designer!

Beyond the hangars and beneath the brilliant Californian sun stand the bigger brethren and some of those still awaiting restoration. Many of the machines have made their way via the famous storage facility of Davis Monthan and still bear evidence of the mothballing designed to preserve them. One such example was within hours of being broken up, a Sikorsky CH-3C, when it was spotted by the Curator of Yanks Museum, who recognised some peculiarities in the paint scheme. One US Commander-in-Chief had the Presidential helicopter changed from Marine's green to the dark blue of his own former service, the Navy. The fateful day in Dallas cut short the Presidency of John F. Kennedy and today the hulk of his helicopter is set to be preserved at Chino.

Chino is all about such history. Perhaps its greatest assets are not merely the hardware, but the stories that the aircraft have brought with them into a new century. Furthermore, by keeping these aircraft flying it allows the sounds, smells and sense of speed of a bygone era to still be with us today. It was a time before wide-bodies and fuel efficiency; it was about pulling 'G' and unadulterated 'grunt'. Somehow static displays don't quite capture that.

Chino is a step back into history and the origins of aviation. Whilst somewhat removed from modern civil aviation, it is a place filled with interest; of fascinating aircraft and the tales of the people who crewed these amazing aircraft. If after taking in the sights and sounds you're still feeling a little unfulfilled, don't forget, there's always coffee and flapjacks at Flo's.

*****

9

Delivering the Mail...100 Years On.

Things weren't looking good.

The next morning, I was scheduled to depart Essendon and re-enact the historic air mail flight undertaken by Maurice Guillaux in 1914. As I sat in my air-conditioned hotel room and logged onto the digital service to find that the weather forecast seemed endless with 'cloud on the ground' at critical locations and line after line of low cloud and heavy rain. I flicked the pages on my iPad between the weather radars for Mount Gambier and Melbourne, endeavouring to get a clearer picture of the waves of water blowing in from the south-west. Was there a possible route out of Melbourne to the west with lower hills and a higher cloud base? I entered in alternate flight plans on the iPad App and compared how much extra time such a plan would cost and then converted that into fuel; there were viable options available. Still, the best news came from the MSL synoptic charts on the Bureau of Meteorology website. Maybe, just maybe, there will be a window of opportunity between the two deep cold fronts that threatened to ruin the centenary air mail flight.

And then I paused...

I had a world of information at my fingertips, mobile phones and mass media. 100 years ago, Guillaux had none of this and yet he set out from Melbourne bound for Sydney in his Bleriot monoplane; exposed to the elements and a simple railway line as his navigation system. On board were 1785 commemorative postcards and Australia's first air freight – orange juice and tea. His weather forecast was his line of sight through the spinning propeller. I had it easy.

It became even easier when the rain on the roof abated and breaks of blue sky appeared over Melbourne. By the time the many media commitments had been met and departure time loomed, things looked positively hopeful. Furthermore, each stage of the flight would have aircraft flying in company with my Jabiru J230D 'air mail' aircraft. Veteran pilot, Aminta Hennessy, in her Cessna 182 was the support aircraft and offered an IFR alternative should the weather close in. For this stage she would be joined by a CT-4 and a Cessna 172 and all three would depart for me, offering some 'eyes in the sky'. As it transpired, as I climbed overhead Essendon I could see for 100 miles and any reservations that I'd held melted away. The centenary air mail flight was underway.

There is nothing quite as relaxing as flying over open fields with blue sky over head and a big strip of highway and railway line to tell you where to go. In my enclosed cabin with GPS, EFIS and cabin heater, I spared a thought for Guillaux battling turbulence and headwinds, the cold winter slipstream biting at his cheeks. On his journey, relief came when he was swamped by the warmth of the people he met along the way. Over 3 days he landed at Seymour and Wangaratta in

Victoria before crossing the border and making stops at Albury, Wagga Wagga, Harden, Goulburn and the Sydney suburb of Liverpool. His final port of call was Moore Park where he was met by the Governor-General.

This flight would also take three days, although not out of necessity as the Jabiru cruised at a comfortable 120 knots and had 5 hours endurance in its fuel tanks. Along the way I would orbit overhead townships such as Seymour, Euroa, Glenrowan and Moss Vale to recognise their part in the original flight. Still, times had changed and Mangalore would step in for Seymour and Mittagong was added to represent Guillaux's weather aborted attempt to land at Moss Vale. Temora and Benalla were added also on the strength of their local aviation communities. A Moore Park landing was considered, but a Bankstown destination was agreed upon.

The flight was the culmination of 18 months of planning for the Aviation Historical Society of NSW, (AHSA) under the management of Tom Lockley. Along with Judy Rainsford, Anthony Coleiro and an enthusiastic team they had considered everything from carrying another 1785 postcards to organising classic aircraft such as a deHavilland Dragon Rapide and a Wirraway to keep the Jabiru from getting lonely. If only Guillaux had been so fortunate.

With Melbourne and the Kilmore Gap behind, the first stop at Mangalore was made amidst multiple training aircraft and a good many birds. In a trend that was set to continue, the townspeople and media turned out to welcome the air mail troupe with the warmest of welcomes. It was a tremendous start and soon we were all underway again, this time with a Winjeel as a companion.

Fog patches still lingered here and there as I levelled out and the greenness of the paddocks indicated a good amount of rain had been forthcoming this winter, hence the prevalence of birdlife at every turn. Birds of another type were floating down as I passed well clear near Euroa and soon Benalla loomed ahead.

The last of our aircraft to arrive, I was astounded at the array of aircraft parked to meet us. Aside from the military trainers were gliders and tug aircraft and a pristine silver deHavilland Dragon Rapide, complete with "Royal Mail" appropriately emblazoned on its flanks. Marshallers in high-visibility vests guided me in as people and cameras gathered behind them. There was another warm welcome in the museum, kind words and an exchange of gifts before we set ourselves to depart again. Short sectors in the air and short stops on the ground added to the excitement of the day and all the while the skies smiled upon us.

At Wangaratta strong crosswinds challenged us, but we all managed to arrive safely. After a few passes, even the Dragon executed a wonderful landing in trying tailwheel conditions. Here it was time for a sausage sizzle and a coffee to keep the chill of the wind at bay. Again the township had attended in force and an old airline friend was among their number. I had parked the Jabiru into wind, but I still kept one eye on the windsock should the gusts become stronger. In fact, by the time we taxied for Albury, the air had calmed to a constant breeze straight down the runway. I turned left after take-off and looked back at the crowd still lingering on the tarmac before levelling the wings and setting course for Albury.

By the time I was to call Albury control tower, the radio frequency was abuzz. Our aircraft were inbound, other aircraft were departing and an RPT turbo-prop was in the mix. I couldn't get a word in so I decided to loiter with intent and take in the beautiful landscape beneath me until finally my turn came and I joined my fellow pilots by the fuel bowser at Albury. Significantly, the historic Ulver DC-2 from the 1934 air race sat only a short distance away and my thoughts again drifted to Guillaux and the other pioneer aviators.

That night as the temperature dropped, we enjoyed a warm meal at our lodgings before I retired early to review the next day's plans. Sydney was experiencing gale force winds and another cold front was showering Melbourne. Meanwhile the air mail flight sat comfortably in an area of high pressure between the two weather systems. The only consideration was fog the next morning as I turned off the light.And fog there was...and ice. When we arrived at the airport the fog was already beginning to dissipate, but a coating of ice shrouded each and every aeroplane. In our favour was the fact that there was only a couple of hours' flight time today, so a delay would not cause any 'last light' issues. The only complication was the co-ordination of the various organisations meeting us at our ports of call.

Great care was taken to ensure that all of the aircraft were free of ice before long engine runs slowly brought engine temperatures into the green band. The airliners departed Albury with their propeller tips leaving spiralling rings of white vapour in their wake now it was our time.

The short hop across to Wagga was again a matter of following the freeway. I spotted the airfield from some distance out, but I was cheating. I had flown 'bank runs' out Wagga in the 90s and in a note of history my Dad had first soloed there in 1947. On the ground the packed tarmac boasted the Rapide, a Wirraway trainer, a canary Piper

Cub and an Ercoupe among their number. Kenny Love and Andrew Bishop from the Temora Aviation Museum were there and more cups of coffee were gratefully accepted.

Judy, Tom and Tony did what they do so well and brought the significant history behind the event to the gathering with well-chosen words. The enthusiasm was tangible and Tom even managed to secure a ride to Temora in the Wirraway; I was just a tad envious. As the plan dictated, I was the last to depart again and it was the best seat in the house as I watched the array of classic aircraft take to the skies and set course for Temora.

The Temora Aviation Museum is a favourite destination for my family, with a photo of my Dad's shattered fighter cockpit featured on the wall. The museum slid beneath me on the downwind leg before I rolled into a base turn back towards the runway. Woomf! I barely had time to react as 3 large hawks swept past my cockpit. I wondered if Guillaux had dodged so much wildlife on his flight.

As I parked the Jabiru, there were a good many familiar faces in the gathering. Unfortunately, there was not enough time to catch up with folks and wander the Museum's halls. The ice that morning had delayed us and Harden's population was on the phone and waiting. Kenny was to escort us on the last leg of the day and again Tom had scored a ride, this time in the little yellow Cub and I suppressed a slight green tinge of envy.

The Harden airstrip runs the length of the town's racecourse with a bit of a slope and a few bumps along its surface. However, it was the gathering of cars and people that really caught my attention. It seemed that half the population had come to greet the flight. I orbited overhead at the request of the media below before lining up on the orange gravel airstrip. Over the fence and into the landing flare...not again...a bird! I don't know who ducked first but somehow the hawk neither smashed into my windscreen nor even thump into the tailplane. I rocked and rolled and considered a go-around, but finally with the wings level I eased the little Jabiru back to earth for an exciting arrival.

The array of aircraft now sat lined up on the racecourse, complemented by a formation flying team from Canberra and an antique Avro Cadet. Following the formalities, the good people of Harden crossed the fence-line and mingled with the pilots and aeroplanes with a good many children securing the opportunity to sit in a cockpit for the first time. The sense of community was everywhere.

Harden had been integral on the flight in 1914 as Guillaux's aborted attempts reach Goulburn had seen him stay there for more than the single night we would be hosted. Even so, we dined and slept in the Carrington Hotel. The very same lodgings where the Frenchman had stayed 100 years before. Over dinner mention was made of a marker that the citizens of Harden had created to aid Guillaux in finding their town and that we would be able to see it the next morning. For now, it was time to rest and ready ourselves for the final day.

Harden's marker for Guillaux was a circle of concrete that now lies near the school under the eyes of the grazing cattle. Almost forgotten it is a silent testament to the significance of the event of a century before. A mere sprinkling of lime in a circle or a fire would not suffice and the town had been determined to create a substantial signal to the French pilot. As I stood in the circle with other members of the air mail group, I truly felt a sense of history about the place.

When we arrived at the aircraft, the ice on the wings was even thicker than the night before at Albury. Once again we waited and wiped until the airframes were clear and clean but now we were behind schedule for the grand finale at Bankstown.

Harden now farewelled us and a short time later Goulburn greeted us. Local dignitaries, antique cars and ladies in period dress set the tone for a warm but whirlwind stop. The efforts of the community were astounding and I sighted an elder statesman in a wheelchair with a pair of RAAF wings sewn to his jacket. I made a point of chatting with him, for the people and not merely the aeroplanes along the way had stories of our nation's aviation heritage.

The crowd at Mittagong rivalled Harden, but was not a total surprise. It is my home airfield and I had been receiving text massages at Goulburn asking about my arrival time and reminding me not to make a mess of the landing. Fortunately, I didn't and I was greeted by the hugs of my wife and kids and a long line of interested onlookers. And again, they had the chance to be up close and personal with aircraft that included the beautifully restored Aero 145.

Yet another cup of coffee later I was on the way with a deHavilland 'Beaver' ahead and Chris Byrne flying the Aero over my shoulder. Over Picton I was joined by the Channel 9 helicopter that went onto shadow my flightpath for the remaining miles to Bankstown. The camera lens glinted outside the helicopter's open door and the sun started to slip lower on the opposite side of the Jabiru.

Within minutes I was crossing the runway threshold at Bankstown

Airport and three days of absolute enjoyment was drawing to a close. I parked the Jabiru and climbed out to be met by the French Consul General, French guards in period costume and an array of media representatives. All too soon the flight was now over.

It was Bastille Day and that night we delivered the air mail ceremoniously to the French and government dignitaries that had come together at the Powerhouse Museum. Specially addressed letters I had been handed by officials in Melbourne were now handed over to their counterparts in Sydney. A good deal of French champagne was flowing and there was genuine pride shown in their countryman who had achieved this memorable flight in the Antipodes.

Hanging from the roof was Guillaux's original Bleriot monoplane that had made the flight so many years ago. As I looked at it I contemplated how far we had come in a century and how much more difficult the journey had been for the brave Frenchman. I had followed Maurice Guillaux's lead, but we were worlds apart in the challenges that were faced. Still it was a flight I will always remember. The chance to carry the air mail....100 years on.

*****

10

The Big Bang

Living in a caravan, pre-dawn pre-flights and a fast-filling logbook. As a young commercial pilot in the Kimberleys life was pretty good, even when things didn't go quite to plan.

Kununurra was full of young pilots and the motto was, "Need a pilot; shake a tree." Fortunately I was able to gain employment with one of the two main charter operators whose fleet consisted of all marques of Cessna singles, a 310, 'push-pull' 337 and a Piper Chieftain. Unquestionably, the workhorses were our Cessna 210s and 206s that ranged far and wide across the remote outback.

Our tasks were many and varied. As daylight first appeared, our convoy of aircraft would convey bus-loads of tourists on scenic flights over Lake Argyle to the bee-hive shaped Bungle Bungle Ranges, returning before the convective turbulence bubbled up in the increasing heat. Charters and the occasional instructional flight filled the remainder of the day and it was not unusual to fly four or five flights in a variety of aircraft. At the end of the day, with aircraft cleaned and fuelled, the mob of like-minded young pilots made their way to their local watering holes. It was General Aviation heaven.

With less than 1,000 hours experience, I had been with the company about six weeks and had already had flown about 100 hours in the company's diverse operations. Over half of that time had been accumulated in the Cessna 210 and on this particular day I had already flown the morning scenic flight, a staff training hop to Lissadell Diamond Mine and a charter to Port Keats, 400km south of Darwin on the Northern Territory side of the border. To finish the day, I had one more run to 'Keats'; easy enough, about an hour each way.

The run was a regular charter to the Aboriginal township where we knew the locals by name. The trip up was without event and after offloading the freight in the mandatory heat and humidity, I waved goodbye and taxied out for the short sector back to Kununurra. Rather than a straight line home, we always flew south to Fossil Head, across to Quoin Island and then directly to Kununurra. This allowed us to cross the Bonaparte Gulf while keeping land within gliding range at all times and avoiding the less than attractive option of ditching in the crocodile and shark filled waters.

At the top of climb I leveled off in the cooler air and attended to the standard routine of cockpit duties. With the engine leaned out and temperatures and pressures in the green, I sat up and enjoyed the beautiful scenery that extended in all directions. The strutless high-wing of the '210 afforded a tremendous view as the sun started to slip toward the western horizon and stretch the shadows beneath me. These were golden days.

Over Quoin Island I changed heading towards Kununurra before lowering my eyes momentarily to complete the Navigation Log. I was penciling in my times across the log when...

Bang!

The bang was accompanied by a physical thud that got my attention very quickly. My eyes sprung up and I scanned outside, with my first thought being a bird-strike. I looked around for evidence of blood and guts or bent metal, but there was none, rather a low vibration through the aeroplane. Still thinking I may have hit a piece of Kimberley wildlife I craned my head back over my shoulder and assessed the tailplane as best I could; nothing apparent.

Drawing my eyes back in and desperately trying to avoid tunnel vision, I scanned the instrument panel for any signs of abnormality. The manifold pressure gauge was quivering and seemed to be reading a little higher if anything. Mind you, the whole aeroplane was quivering a little. Exercising the throttle seemed to worsen the vibration, so I smoothly returned it to its previous setting. I now suspected an engine problem, but was unable to trouble shoot any obvious cause. I decided to exercise the final stage of aviate-navigate-communicate and contacted Flight Service by radio. I advised them of my undiagnosed dilemma and revised my arrival time at Kununurra as I seemed to have lost a little groundspeed. All the while I scanned for potential landing fields below in case things went pear-shaped quickly.

Hearing my radio call, a nearby company aircraft made his way to my position about 40 nautical miles from home. The other Cessna closed to a safe distance 'up sun', but could see nothing wrong. He then formated to port, but admitted he could see very little as my aircraft was now silhouetted against the rapidly setting sun. We flew in loose formation until Kununurra appeared ahead, at which time my partner accelerated away and set about putting his aircraft on the ground.

For my part, I decided to maintain my present altitude until I reached the airfield as height equates to time and options in a single engine aircraft. Fortunately, the land around Kununurra was forced landing friendly if I needed to put the Cessna down in a hurry. I secured any loose items in the cockpit and completed my pre-landing checks as I approached overhead. I now received my first positive indication of the problem; the oil pressure was beginning to drop.

I advised Flight Service of my intentions to join overhead before flying a descending left-hand circuit onto Runway 12. It was now right on dusk as I turned back to join a close crosswind. The oil pressure was now sinking even lower and the other engine instruments began to go out in sympathy. With the now-lit runway right below I selected gear down and began to configure the aircraft for the approach to land. The oil temperature now began to rise rapidly, so with a landing assured I shutdown the engine, pulling the throttle and mixture in succession.

Putting the glide approach to real use rather than training, I aimed well into the runway and lowered the final flaps as I rounded the corner on a close base leg. With no further need for electrical power, I switched off the 'Master Switch' and lined up on the 1800 metre strip. The landing itself was straightforward and I rolled to a halt on the centerline before shutting down the now-silent Cessna and climbing out. As I closed the door, I felt my hand slip from the handle. On turning around I was stunned; the entire port side of the aircraft was coated in oil. I could now safely rule out a bird-strike!

Towed back to the hangar, the engine cowls were removed to show the cause of my drama. A cylinder-head on the Continental IO-520 engine had separated. I was amazed at the degree of the damage, yet the aircraft had continued to perform. Until the last few minutes when the oil pressure had fallen, the symptoms had been mild with only an underlying vibration at cruise power settings. To the credit of my employer, he grounded the fleet immediately and inspected all of the similarly-engined Cessnas for any warning signs of an impending failure.

As a young inexperienced commercial pilot, the cylinder-head separation had me guessing until the engine cowls were finally lifted off inside the hangar. I thought about what I might have done differently and had a good chat with our engineers. Curiously, it seemed that as pilots we were always training for total engine failures, total hydraulic failures, total electrical failures and the like. However, more often the incidents are partial failures with insidious symptoms that sometimes develop into a major, total failure. It was real food for thought for a young aviator.

Finally, it was off to the watering hole before a very good night's sleep. After all, the next day I had charters to fly across some of Australia's most beautiful scenery. As I said, as a young commercial pilot in the Kimberleys life was pretty good, even when things didn't go quite to plan.

*****

The cause of the "Big Bang". A separated cylinder head on my Cessna 210

The impressive N3N, complete with 'planter', at Chino, California.

61

11

Wings of Hope

Every day there seems to be a reminder of the devastating power of Mother Nature. Her brute force is varied and does not discriminate, with the potential to level cities and bring nations to their knees. Yet amidst these tragedies we are also reminded of how the world can come together as one in a way that seems to defy every other global circumstance. Physical and fiscal aid brushes away borders and humanity is able to be recognised for its redeeming qualities rather than its recklessness.

When natural disasters strike, aviation has a key role to play. The machine that owes much of its whirlwind evolution to times of war is now the primary means of rapid response for those in trouble. Whether the situation is an international crisis or a lone stranded hiker in an inaccessible canyon, aircraft can provide assistance in a manner and time-frame that can only come from the skies.

The first recorded air-sea rescue dates back to 1911 when a Curtiss seaplane undertook a rescue sortie on Lake Michigan in the United

States. In 1917, Australian Frank McNamara won the Victoria Cross when he landed his Martynside bomber under enemy fire to rescue a downed fellow pilot after a raid near Gaza. And so, the seeds of airborne rescue were sown, growing in complexity at a rate corresponding to the development of the machines. Aircraft as simple as Tiger Moths had their rear fuselage modified to accommodate a stretcher and patient while the remarkable Douglas C-47, became a stalwart of allied medical evacuations in World War Two. Yet perhaps the most significant development saw the advent of the helicopter. Its ability to hover above and extract patients from a small clearing or disabled vessel rather than a prepared runway immediately ear-marked the helicopter as a key player in the rescue field. From the close of World War Two to the present day, helicopters have been at the forefront of this vital role.

It was also in war that the logistics of moving men, supplies and machines grew to a grand scale. Legends emerged such as the airborne crossing of the Himalayan Mountains, or 'Flying the Hump'. With seaborne routes blocked, China was supplied from the air to enable it to continue its war with the Japanese. From 1942 and in the face of towering terrain and horrendous weather, over 600 aircraft were ultimately lost flying this dangerous yet critical route. From a 'Cold War' perspective, the Berlin Airlift bypassed the Soviet blockade of the city from the air to provide the supplies needed by its isolated occupants. Over the 11 month blockade more than 200,000 flights were conducted and ultimately resulted in continued access from the West being afforded to Berlin.

In the current day, the use of aircraft in humane endeavours is highly diversified and far-reaching. The range and speed of modern transport aircraft have indeed shrunk the world in a commercial sense, but this technology also permits the rapid deployment of aid. Tragedies such as the Haiti Earthquake and the Indonesian Boxing Day Tsunami have resulted in a response from all corners of the globe and not merely the immediate neighbours of the stricken nations. Such is the speed with which assistance can be mobilised, that initial response rescue teams can be on-scene within hours to help in the search for survivors. This is then followed by the co-ordinated supply of food, water and shelter on a scale that could not be imagined before the advent of the aeroplane.

In the face of fire, aircraft now battle hot-spots from the air. Whether it is via a 'Bambi-Bucket' tethered beneath a helicopter, a converted Boeing 747 with a 20,000 US Gallon tank or deploying fire-fighters at the fire-front, airborne resources provide a real tactical advantage against bush-fires. The aircraft's speed can permit an early response to a small remote outbreak before it escalates, while their precision can dump retardant within metres of battling fire crews and threatened homes. In contrast, when communities are isolated by rising flood waters, helicopters can provide rescue and the vast tailgates of military transport aeroplanes can deploy food for man and livestock from above.

Organisations such as Australia's Royal Flying Doctor Service have been providing aero-medical transport for over ninety years and now such services have almost become an expectation of modern society. Whether retrieving critically ill accident victims or routinely transporting patients from remote communities to the advanced facilities in major centres, air transport provides a timely, comfortable means of transfer for those already suffering.

When oil rigs catch alight or vessels are lost miles from home, relief comes from the air. Air forces and civil operators boast the range and technology to locate and recover stranded victims despite foul weather or the difficulty of the extrication. From large fixed-wing electronic surveillance marvels to small rotary-wing aircraft and the unique skills of their remarkable crews, there are very few situations when the skies cannot provide both the most rapid search capability and subsequent transfer to safety.

The spectacular performance of the modern fighter jet is always the drawcard for any air display. Yet at times such as when the Haitian community is devastated to a level beyond comprehension it is worth recalling the many noble roles that the aircraft has undertaken across the years. The very nature of aviation's freedom in the three dimensions allows it to access disasters with speed when other means of communication and contact are cut. Task specific helicopters and aeroplanes have even dispensed with the need for a runway in many instances as winches and aerial deployment of loads provide immediate aid. We must also remember those who crew these aircraft. Not just the pilots, but the winch operators, crewmen, doctors, nurses, loadmasters and paramedics. Their skill, care and compassion are the factors that transform an inert machine to a life saving resource.

Aviation has brought our world closer together in so many ways. Yet undoubtedly the most worthy pursuit of aviation is in the way that we can help each other and enhance our ability to co-exist. Even in its darkest hours, the world can take comfort in the knowledge that at an airfield somewhere, there is always a crew at the ready with their wings of hope.

*****

12

Home Again.

As I walk around the jet with my torch in hand, there is bustling activity in every quarter. Engineers attend to paperwork and containers are being loaded into cargo holds as the refuelling truck pumps its precious fluid into the wings. The noise filters through my hearing protection as I methodically work my way around the aircraft and even after so many years, I am impressed by the choreography of an airliner transit; particularly now. For it is the middle of the night and I stand on the opposite side of the country to my sleeping family, but here, there is no time for slumber. The job is only half done.

It is a hot, summer night and the humidity is tangible. My shirt sticks to my back and condensation drips from the underside of the wing beneath the cool jet fuel within. Climbing the steps, the passengers are not far behind. The cabin is cool and almost eerie as the air-conditioned air pours from the vents like a cascading mist. On the flight-deck, my fellow pilot works his way through his duties.

Ground staff shuttle between the aircraft and their office, while our displays affirm that the cargo holds are now closed. The clock is counting down and the final forms are signed and the briefings completed. The final door is closed, the stairs pull away and we are ready for departure. For the second time tonight, the tug pushes us back from the terminal and one after the other, the engines are brought to life with fuel, air and ignition. The ground crew waves and the tug drives off before we receive clearance and begin the trek back home.

As we taxi into the darkness, the lights of the airport fade complex behind us and just the greens and blues of taxiways shine up from beneath. Above, the sky is an infinite sea of stars on the very blackest of backdrops. When the time is right, we once more advance the thrust levers and feel the reassuring push into our seats. Our speed increases and the airflow breathes life into the inert metal of our wings. The roar of the engines, the rumbling of the wheels. And then flight.

The noise and seemingly the rest of humanity falls away as we move from one realm to another. The noise and activity of the transit is replaced by the rushing airflow and as switch off the last of our landing lights, we merge with the darkness and set course for the stars. Ahead, very distant flashes of light resemble old footage of artillery barrages at night, but these are nature's guns in the form of nocturnal thunderstorms. Perhaps we will be lucky tonight and the storms will keep their distance?

We settle into the cruise and check the weather for the airports along the way. We have nearly exhausted our conversation and just the occasional exchange between us and the dim glow of the instrument panel differentiates us from the darkness outside. Home is out there in that darkness, hours away and too far to see.

The night has been long and quiet.

The hum of the engines has become rhythmic and bordering on hypnotic in these small hours. Compared to the hustle and bustle of the ground crews administering their tasks, our jet now seems to be a solitary soul. That departure is now a memory - our destination grows slowly closer as the miles countdown and those same stars continue their arc across the sky.

At times, towering cumulus clouds have been scattered left and right of our path y, reaching high above our flight deck. Some have been illuminated by the brightest of moons, while others have had their fuse lit within, erupting in broad sheets and jagged earthbound spikes. Occasionally, St. Elmo's fire has crept up the windscreen with its tiny shards mimicking the massive electric claws of the sky around us. But soon they too have faded and all that is left is the darkness below and the sea of stars overhead. Fortunately, the storms have kept their distance.

At first the horizon glows and is no more than a hint of the day to come. And then dawn fades into a thin orange band trapped between cloud layers and in limbo between day and night. All the while, the engines hum.

The passengers begin to stir beyond the flight deck door and shifting galley carts join the shuffling footsteps to provide further evidence that the night is nearly over. The once near-silent radio increases its tempo as clearances are issued to the inbound flights, converging on the harbour city from all directions and distant lands.

Day is now pushing the night from its home. Its stars begin to dim and the black sky now turns grey. Only in the land of nod below does night still reign, gathered in by shadows and tinged with the lights of highways. Most of the land is still asleep as we begin our descent through the twilight to the last remaining traces of the evening.

As we pass through a thin layer of expansive cloud, it draws a line like a water level with bubbling clouds bursting through as if they are ice bergs in the sky. Above, they are white and lit by the dawn, while below they are still grey and seemingly menacing. We step left and right with respect, hurtling through imaginary valleys of clear air and further into the darkness. But the day must win as it always does.

The sun casts its rays and the night retreats. As the dark shroud slips back, the terrain grows in character and shadows begin to be cast. The water ahead is glassy and mirrors the sky in both texture and stillness. The calm of the morning is only broken by the slow, strong flashing light that sweeps the horizon with precision. It is the beacon of the airport and like the night our job is nearly done. We are home again.

*****

13

Just Another Town

It's late in the day. The sun is back over my shoulder and the last rays of light are glowing around the winglet of the Boeing 737, giving it the appearance of a lone memorial at dusk. The low hum of the airflow moving past the windscreen at three-quarters of the speed of sound provides the background music, while the lyrics punch out sporadically over the VHF radio. I'm at 37,000 feet, the air is smooth and all is good with the world.

Back in the darkened cabin the passengers have dined and now recline their seats in an effort to steal a few precious moments of slumber; they are also comforted by the humming, glassy-smooth air. The west coast of Australia is two hours behind and the east lies a couple ahead. The waters of the Great Australian Bight have been crossed and the glow of lights begins to appear far below. Coastal hamlets and fishing ports mainly, their vessels unloading the days haul as their fireplaces are stoked up in anticipation of the cool night ahead.

All the while the navigation display reassures us that we are not lost above this island continent. The small triangle that represents the aeroplane continues to track steadily along the magenta line that leads us home, while other numbers and arrows tell us about the frozen world of the upper atmosphere outside. The letters MTG start to move down the 'nav display' as we grow closer to the township that bears those letters. As I squint in the fading light I can see yet another glow, more substantial than the coastal villages, but still far from the blazing lights of the cities. It's a rural township and one that I have come to know over the years; it is Mount Gambier.

From Flight Level 370, it is just another town and yet it's not. I cast my mind back to my childhood when I clambered over aeroplanes at Mount Gambier and explored the old hangars and weatherboard huts that had taken shape in the dark days of World War Two. My father had been posted there for a short period in the Air Force when he was little more than a boy. A young sun-drenched Queenslander in the cold, wet winter of the South Australian coast-line, he shivered at the memory and pointed out the very awnings under which he took shelter in his bulky woollen coat and forage cap. A canvas kit bag of possessions slung over his shoulder, the days ahead were a mystery to him back then and life in wartime held little certainty. Thirty years later, his greatest fear was that I would fall from the precarious looking structure that I was attempting to climb as all young boys do. In my mind I can still see him surveying the place that he once called home and feel his strong-scarred hands lifting me back down to safety.

"Climb to Flight Level 390!" The radio squawks and I am in the present, but the call is not for my aircraft and I lean forward to watch Mount Gambier draw closer.

Twenty years beyond boyhood and I am at Mount Gambier again. This time the weather is foul and I am letting down through the thrashing rain in a small twin-engined aeroplane. To my right sits the girl that I would marry, although at that time the odds seemed pretty long that would happen. I can hardly hear the sound of the undercarriage extending above the racket created by the pelting rain on the windscreen. Gradually the earth comes into view and then features consistent with an airport. Buffeted by the winds, I manoeuvre the machine to line up with the runway and finally exhale as the wheels touch down safely on the drenched asphalt.

In suit and tie, I lash down the aeroplane while my future bride-to-be organises a taxi cab. As the rain finally ceases, I am distracted and ill at ease; I have made trips like this too many times over the course of my career. The cab comes to a halt; I pay the fare and begin to walk reluctantly. Either side of me stand the headstones and graves of passed souls. Ahead is the Mount Gambier crematorium where my mate lies waiting to make his final journey; another young pilot whose luck ran out. I steel myself, lock my jaw and bury every fibre of emotion in the manner that my father instilled in me from an early age. It is a skill that served him well in combat and me in my time as a paramedic. The only thing I truly feel is frustration at the tragic waste of another young life.

Tonight the lights of Mount Gambier slip beneath the nose of my Boeing and I bid it adieu until the next time I cross the continent. Today it is a waypoint on a flight-plan, but in the past this town left its mark on me. Like every other town I see loom on the horizon before disappearing beyond the tail in a heartbeat, it has a story to tell. The story may not always be one that I know or can even grasp at such a great height; nonetheless, its people and its history are treasures in their own rights. I am just a traveller using their lights to guide my way as I tip-toe past the fringe of their world in the night. But now it is gone and another town makes its way towards me. It is another piece of this great land and another piece of my journey aloft. And although the line of lights can sometimes seem endless, never will I look upon their glow as merely just another town.

*****

14

One More Time With Feeling.

When QANTAS received their first Boeing 767 in 1985, Ronald Regan was the US President and Kirrily Zupp was starting high school. Over the ensuing 29 years the political landscape would change, but the 767 would remain a reliable constant for airlines around the world.

The aircraft would also become a central figure in the life of Kirrily Zupp. The daughter of a former air force and QANTAS pilot, she had aspired to fly for the 'Flying Kangaroo' since childhood. Given her chance in 1996, she first flew as a Second Officer on the Boeing 747-400 before the opportunity arose to upgrade to a First Officer on the 767 in the year 2000.

After 3 months of classrooms, simulators and theory training, she first flew the 767 in May. The flight was a series of circuits at Avalon designated as 'Base Training' in which the most recent trainees were given their first taste of the 767. Without passengers on board it was an eye-opening introduction to the twin-engined Boeing and its stunning take-off performance. This was an impressive aspect of the 767 that would remain with Kirrily for the next 15 years.

Those circuits at Avalon were just the beginning. Over the decades, the QANTAS Boeing 767 fleet included 'extended range' -200s and -300s powered by both Rolls Royce and General Electric engines and rarely were they operated at their stellar performance limits. Consequently, it seemingly leapt into the sky and came to a halt easily with its brakes designed to stop a far more laden aircraft. These were just a couple of features that endeared the 767 to its crews as a 'pilot's aeroplane' and yet it was equally enamoured by business and leisure travellers alike.

On a daily basis, Kirrily and her fellow crews would ply the domestic network across the length and breadth of Australia. Beyond the home shores there were also a range of international destinations with Asia featuring heavily. Hong Kong, Singapore, Manila, Narita, and Taipei were just some the ports with Kirrily also managing one flight to Bali. The 'Bombay Shuttle' operated between Singapore and Mumbai, while Honolulu was always a favoured transit. Closer to home, day trips to New Zealand and Noumea were regular occurrences while the night saw back-of-clock freighter services crossing the Tasman and the 767 filling yet another important role.

As well as places, people also featured heavily in Kirrily's time on the 767. She shared the flight deck with a range of great crews over nearly fifteen years on the aircraft, but there were interesting folks in the cabin as well. Russell Crowe, Delta Goodrem, national leaders, television cast members and sports stars added to the interest of another day at the office. Surprisingly, even in the 21st century, celebrities and the general public alike still seemed particularly interested in the concept of a female airline pilot.

Times change. Since Kirrily's first circuits at Avalon in 2000 until 2014, the 767 fleet had covered many, many miles and delivered millions of passengers safely to their loved ones. In that time Kirrily had brought her own four little 'passengers' into the world and re-trained on the 767 each time that she returned to work. In many ways, the 767 had also become a part of her family.

Now the inevitable march of time had heralded the 767s retirement. 2014 had seen a number of the type retired and ferried to Victorville in the United States and the growing facility at Alice Springs to await their varied fates. Kirrily had watched one such flight featured on '60 Minutes' but personally held a desire to fly the last commercial service. She was now the longest serving First Officer on the aircraft and hoped that her seniority would permit her to crew the final flight.

When the final flying rosters were released she was thrilled to see her name paired for QF452 on December 27th. The Pilot-in-Command was to be the QANTAS Head of Flying Operations, Captain Mike Galvin and two other First Officers, Joe Reitemann and Rohan Flick would assist the operation from the flight deck's 'jump seats'.

In time the flight number was changed to the more appropriate QF767 and behind the scenes a good deal of organisation was underway to make the flight something special. The 767 had struck a chord with passengers over the years and now aviation enthusiasts lined up to book their seats on the final service. Among the passengers were two special names, Bob Bishop and Dave Macintyre. Both had recently retired after flying the 767 since its introduction and now they had bought tickets to say their own farewell to a trusted friend.

When December 27th arrived, Kirrily set off from home to fly the 767 for the final time and arrived at flight briefing well and truly early. For the penultimate sector from Sydney to Melbourne, Kirrily would be the flying pilot, while Mike would have the honour on the last flight.

In the lead up to the day, Kirrily had been asked by a good many people how she felt about the retirement of the 767 and her final flight. As departure time now closed in, the emotions were mixed. There was a sense of sentimentality about saying goodbye to an aircraft that had featured so significantly in her career, but her greater focus was on making sure that the flight went well.

Arriving at the gate lounge at Sydney, there was already a buzz. A good many passengers had purchased tickets both to and from Melbourne and the excitement had already begun to brew. The crew were stopped and asked to have their photos taken or come in closer for a 'selfie'. It was apparent that this wasn't simply another flight.

As Kirrily raised the 767's nose into the air for the final time and navigated the way to Melbourne, the event was being recorded on the flight deck through a series of cameras. New South Wales and Victoria slipped beneath the nose before VH-OGL, the 'City of Wangaratta' pitched into descent for the second last time. The scene was very familiar for the crew as they manoeuvred to land on Melbourne's Runway 16 and despite the watching eyes of the Go-Pro cameras, she eased the wheels smoothly back to earth for the last time. That in itself was a great relief.

The scene at Melbourne Airport was incredible. As the crew emerged from the aerobridge and into the lounge area, they were met by a sea of people and flashing cameras. Media crews jostled for position and questions flew thick and fast. QANTAS had allowed a 2-hour transit between the flights and at this time it seemed that every minute would be needed. Aviation enthusiasts from around the country had descended on Melbourne to be a part of the final flight.

Mike, Kirrily, Joe and Rohan were asked to pose in a constant stream of photographs with smiling passengers and sign boarding passes and all manner of 767 memorabilia. Meanwhile Mike fielded the mainstream media's questions about the aeroplane and what the day truly meant. The scene was more reminiscent of a celebrity's hotel foyer than an airline terminal prior to boarding.

Kirrily was very humbled by the attention being bestowed upon her. As she looked around at the sheer enthusiasm of the gathered crowd she was overwhelmed by the passion of the people for aviation and on this day, the 767. At that moment she felt extremely proud and privileged to be involved in QF767.

Ultimately, the crew had to leave the passengers at the lounge and ready the aircraft, just as they had done many times before, but there was no mistaking that this time was special. For Kirrily, the thought kept surfacing that "this is the last time". The last time to calculate take-off data, the last time to move this switch on the overhead panel, the last time to read this checklist. It was a familiar process tinged with finality.

Meanwhile in the cabin, the mood was one of excitement. Each passenger was greeted by a bag full of QANTAS mementoes including a specially printed T-shirt commemorating the final flight. The cabin crew further fostered the sense of celebration as QF767 pushed back to depart for the very last time.

An arch of water cannons farewelled the flight at Melbourne, although their aim actually just missed the aircraft. Cameras lined the airfield perimeter as the Boeing lined up at the full length of Runway 16. The aeroplane obviously didn't require the 3 kilometres to become airborne, but the use of the runway facilitated better access for the many cameras that were trained in the direction of QF767.

Under Mike's steady hand the thrust levers advanced for the last time...and then they were away. Kirrily raised the landing gear upon Mike's command and the Boeing roared into the sky before turning right and setting course northbound. Air Traffic Control bid them farewell and the final QANTAS 767 had officially departed.

The flight time to Sydney was only a little over an hour and yet a QANTAS engineer managed to squeeze in a marriage proposal. And receive an acceptance. The passengers were making the most of their last goodbye as the crew were cleared to descend off the coast of Sydney and overfly the city's spectacular harbour. For nearly half an hour the 767 waved goodbye to Sydney, all the while being filmed by hovering helicopters and earthbound iPhones. By midnight the internet would be abuzz with thousands of images of the aircraft and its crew as social media transmitted and tweeted.

On the flight deck, the focus remained on keeping the operation safe amidst the excitement. Finally, the time had come to fly that last vector and intercept the final approach for the final time. As Mike configured the landing gear and flaps, Kirrily selected the levers and made the calls just as she had done thousands of time before. As in Melbourne, Air Traffic Control were as warm with their greetings as they were with their clearances.

The runway now loomed large and the computer-generated voice of the Radio Altimeter counted down the final feet of flight. And then it was done. Mike rolled the 767 smoothly onto runway 16 Right as the spoilers deployed and the reverse thrust burst into life. Exiting the runway, Kirrily spoke to the surface movement controller as she 'cleaned up' the flaps and systems deployed for the last landing.

Approaching the parking bay, the water cannons sprayed their arch, creating a misty rainbow in the process. This time they found their mark and doused the 767 from flight deck to fin as she made her way to the gate. Park brake on, engines off, beacon off....it was done.Kirrily completed her checks twice, determined not to make an omission on this very last occasion. Then as the aircraft fell silent, she allowed herself to feel a little emotional for the first time as the aircraft and passengers had now safely arrived.

Mike made his way from the flight deck to individually farewell the passengers as Kirrily was left to contemplate the flight deck. She was going to miss the 767 and reflected how it could do just about anything. It could carry passengers or freight just about anywhere and still carry huge amounts of fuel. It was wonderful to handle and its performance was impressive to say the very least. Simply put, she loved flying the 767.

Looking up she could see her four children waving vigorously from within the terminal. She cracked the cockpit window open and waved backed; now they jumped up and down with excitement. Her kids raced to meet her when she finally arrived in the gate lounge and the cameras continued to click and capture the moment. Everywhere passengers gathered in their 767 'Final Flight' T-Shirts and recounted details of the magic of that last service. More photographs, more autographs and still more interviews. Slowly the crowd dissipated and merged with other passengers about the terminal. On the ground, engineers moved around the tarmac in small groups looking at the flanks of the 767 like a racehorse recently retired.

Kirrily took her family down to see the 767 one last time before it was towed away from the gate. They were each introduced to 'Captain Mike' before they saw the flight deck first hand. Kirrily's 5-year-old son was in awe of the sea of switches and lights. She explained to him that this was her aeroplane and that it had just flown it last flight. He paused, looked around and spoke, "Mum, I want to be a pilot. Tell me what every switch does."

In 2014, Barack Obama was the US President and Hayden Zupp was about to start school.

Farewell QF767.

*****

15

Even Greater Leaps

For many, July in 2009 may have come and gone like any other with Christmas looming ever closer on the horizon. For those of us with a penchant for aviation, the month saw the marking of two significant anniversaries; 100 years since Bleriot's crossing of the English Channel and 40 years since Armstrong and Aldrin first set foot on the moon. Aviation has undoubtedly set the pace for development over the last hundred or so years. It has come through a great deal of sacrifice on the part of many and the pioneering efforts of a brave few. As a consequence the barriers of scale, speed and sound have been broken with ever increasing frequency. But is that pioneer spirit dead today? Lost in a world of computers, comfort and convenience?

There is no doubting the efforts and endurance of the likes of Lindbergh, Hinkler and Henshaw. Cramped cockpits, deafening noise, sleep deprivation and loneliness were only some of the hurdles the early globetrotters faced. I recently wandered through Bert Hinkler's relocated English home and could almost hear the walls speak. His great planning and enroute navigation system was nothing more than a copy of 'The Times Atlas'.

Today, the challenges are far different for the modern pioneers. True, they are the beneficiaries of evolved technology and enhanced communications, but there are still a number of unknowns when venturing far beyond the regular comfort zone. Furthermore, Mother Nature and her potentially brutal skies are as heinous as they ever were and regardless of aircraft design, respect must still be paid.

One only has to look at Chalkie Stobbart's recent assault on Henshaw's Cape Town to London and return record. Sure the technology was there, but it was still a lone man in a single engine aircraft covering a vast portion of the globe. Any number of things could have gone wrong with potentially drastic consequences. As with the pioneers of yesteryear, thorough preparation and sheer determination will go a long way towards overcoming many of the challenges that may arise. And one can bet that the global 'red tape' is rather more complex now than it was in the early days.

As an industry, we face the challenges of an increasingly environmentally sensitive world and in response the drawing boards are full of plans seeking more efficient answers to existing tasks. The Space Shuttle program has now ceased and alternatives had to be found to support the International Space Station in its absence. So where are our new horizons that call for passion and imagination? The first that comes to mind is a possible manned voyage to Mars.

When the Mars Rovers beamed back images of the red planet, they filled the covers of broadsheets across the world. Immediately the debate and discussion about a manned mission arose. At the Apollo 11 crew reunion, 'Buzz' Aldrin called for a manned mission to one of

Mars' moons and to create a staging point for observations and manned sorties to the surface of the red planet. The man who was once at the sharp end of the space race and kicked lunar dust in 1969 believes that this should be the goal.

Closer to home, Sir Richard Branson's 'Virgin Galactic' seeks to put space within the reach of every man; for a price. Launched from the mother ship, the space tourist will have the opportunity to experience the silence, serenity and absence of gravity on the fringes of space. What was once the domain of Jules Verne's novels could become the ultimate adventure ride for those who can afford the fare. Initially it may be economics that limits the access to such a flight, but no longer will it be merely the stuff of dreams.

Nearer to Mother Earth is the concept of hypersonic transport at speeds in excess of five times the speed of sound. Having blasted skyward and freed itself of our atmosphere, the hypersonic aircraft would shut down its engines before reaching the peak of its climb at around 200,000 feet, pitching over and descending back towards the earth. On reaching the outer limits again, the denser atmosphere and timely firing of engines will 'skip' the craft back into space to repeat the process every few minutes. Skipping around the world at Mach 10 would place any point on the globe only a matter of hours away. Fantasy? The HyperSoar project doesn't seem to think so.

The pioneering spirit is still alive. Whether it is a modern aviator challenging his own limits and those of his aircraft or a new venture into space, the sky is never the limit. Of equal importance is the fact that aviation and aerospace beg us to stir our inner imagination and aspire to the ultimate higher ground. Just as our forefathers may well have looked upon the glowing embers from their first fires drifting upwards into the night sky, we still gaze above with wide eyes and deep breaths.

There are fiscal realities, long term responsibilities and the inevitable regulatory processes to deal with, but they should never impinge on the core human instinct to dream and push the boundaries. Aviation has a proud heritage of pioneers who have done this very thing, often in the face of fierce opposition and ridicule. Whether the challenge lies in a light aircraft crossing the Pacific Ocean or a Mars base station being constructed on Phobos, the spark must come from a human mind and the execution from a sturdy heart. With this combination of the species' best qualities our world can continue to take even greater leaps for mankind.

*****

A dramatic shot of the final QANTAS 767 service.

(Photo: Seth Jaworski).

***

16

Caribous, Cattle and Crossbows

2009 saw the deHavilland Caribous of the Royal Australian Air Force celebrate 45 years of service and ultimately their retirement. In that time they had performed under the most trying of conditions, both at home and abroad. One of its earliest deployments was to Vietnam, where Barrie Brown served as a young Flying Officer. Brown had been diverted to Vietnam enroute from Canada while delivering the RAAF's first Caribous to Australia. Little did he know that within a year he would be back there on active service.

The RAAF Transport Flight Vietnam (RTFV) was based out of Vung Tau, with its pilots accommodated a jeep ride away on the northern bank of the Mekong River. At an earlier time, the villas that now housed the Aussie pilots had formed part of South Vietnam's "French Riviera". In 1965 the contingent, callsign "Wallaby Flight", consisted of 6 aeroplanes and 13 pilots supported by RAAF ground crew. Alongside United States and allied forces, Vung Tau was a hive of activity, with a mass of helicopters and Pilatus Porters doing 'touch and go's' across the runway. Brown recalls, "You could be sixth in line and cleared to land, or cleared for take-off with an aircraft head-on about to land. You'd just take-off and break." "Even so", he adds, "I can't recall any mid-air collisions in my time there. You just kept your eyes open."

The RAAF operation saw four aircraft operating seven days a week, in what Barrie affectionately terms "Milk Runs". With one aircraft operating from Da Nang, the other Caribous headed for Saigon, due south and along the east coast respectively. With most sectors in the vicinity of fifteen minutes and around eight sectors per day, the two pilots and 'loadmaster' became very familiar with their machine and its role. Far from crates of dairy products, Brown recalls a litany of cargo, "Passengers, mail, rice, salt, fish, fish oil, grass mats, bodies and coffins." The vast load often called for crews to take up their stations on board first, with the load subsequently piled up behind them. "We also carried live cattle that were restrained by tie-down straps." Lacking the house manners of normal passengers, the cattle often responded to nature's call requiring the back of the Caribou "to be hosed out post-flight". However, this behaviour was far more bearable than one particular pig's adventure. Barrie relates, "We carried live pigs in cane baskets. I heard of one that got loose from its basket not long after take-off. With the back door open, the pig apparently spotted the light and bolted straight out from a height of a few hundred feet!"

Operations were predominantly flown visually, often below a low cloud base that shrouded the surrounding hills. Whilst terrain was an ever present threat, it was obviously not the sole enemy. The Australians were always at risk from ground fire and flew spiralling approaches accordingly. Brown's aircraft took hits on two occasions.

88

One of these followed the delivery of a 105mm Howitzer into a critically short one-way airstrip. The artillery piece had been broken down into components and, after great effort, loaded into the Caribou. Relieved of the Howitzer, the RAAF crew made ready for departure. "It was situated in a valley, so we used to depart 'on the deck'. It was coming out of there that we took two hits in the belly." On the receiving end was a South Vietnamese soldier. His injuries were not fatal and had been lessened to some degree by "deflector boards" that were fitted to the Caribou just beneath his seat.

Knowing little about Vietnam before leaving Australian shores, the Caribou missions took the young pilot into the South Vietnamese heartlands. Surrounded by jutting hills, lush jungle and watercourses, Brown's strongest memory of his tour of duty is the sheer "beauty of the country". He recalls the missions as 'milk runs' but adds, "There was nothing boring about the flying." Zig-zagging between freighters on approach to the strip at Cam Ranh Bay was exciting, but it was the runway at Ha Tien that was most interesting. Situated on the Mekong Delta, the runway itself had been dug out of a rice paddy. The excavated clay had been dried and 'cooked' before being used for foundation. It was then covered with bamboo poles and topped with Pierced Steel Planking (PSP). Around 1000 feet in length and 40 feet wide, it offered only 4 feet of clearance either side of the Caribou's main landing gear! Crosswind landings were not permitted, though the 'luxury' of a small unloading and turning bay did exist at the airstrip's end. Brown recalls, "The wheels were always in 6 to 8 inches of water. The take-off technique was to wait for the end to disappear under the nose and then rotate. This occurred at about 55 knots."

This airstrip claimed Caribou A4-173, the aircraft that Brown had delivered from Canada the preceding year. In May 1965 as it attempted to land at Ha Tien, "173" touched down short of the strip with devastating effect. The starboard gear sheared and the Caribou collapsed on to its wing and prop causing major damage. A replacement wing was subsequently flown in by helicopter and the aircraft repaired in situ. A novel photo opportunity existed when the aircraft was subsequently flown out with one wing bearing the Australian Kangaroo roundel and the other the 'stars and stripes' of the United States Air Force! Despite the potential for mishap, Brown remembers the challenge of such landing fields as an enjoyable aspect of his time abroad.

Flight into many of these airstrips was for the purpose of resupplying US camps with rations, medical supplies and ammunition. Speaking of their allies, Brown states, "Relations with the Americans was generally good, especially with the guys in the field. A typical camp had two or three 'Yanks' and a hundred South Vietnamese or Montagnard troops." The Americans would always offer the Aussies lunch and the latter were only too happy to oblige. Curiously, another aspect to the relationship hinged around the return of empty bottles for cash deposits. "We used to return their 'empties'. Their own blokes didn't seem to care, but it was no problem for us to throw the bottles in the Caribou and take them back. As a consequence, we were extremely well received."

The Montagnard, or "Mountain People", was another ally. Brown remembers them as being a good people; short, tough and "very anti communist". They possessed small crossbows that were incredibly tightly strung and would fire a 12 inch bamboo arrow. In his room one evening Brown attempted to relieve the boredom by shooting the arrow into the thick wooden door of his villa apartment. "It went straight through the bloody door! It was incredibly powerful." Left jutting from the other side, the arrowhead fortunately caused no damage to life or limb. Though not fired again, the crossbow did make the long journey home to Australia.

The RTFV did not have the airspace to itself. An absence of radar and prevalence of cloud meant that aircraft were not always aware of each others' presence. "On one sortie I saw a Canberra dive down in front of us," he starts, "and then another and another." Brown describes the looping motion of the bombers using his hands in the best fighter-pilot fashion. "I had flown through the middle of a Canberra bombing raid!" At times, being on the ground wasn't any safer. "At one of the bigger bases, I think it was NhaTrang," Brown strains his memory banks, "I was waiting to take-off when a South Vietnamese A1 Skyraider landed on its belly tank right in front of me. The whole aeroplane went up in flames." Miraculously, the pilot, escaped without a scratch. Faced with an obvious delay and readying to offer assistance, the Aussie crew shutdown their Caribou. As fire tenders whizzed by, the Tower called the 'Wallaby' to 'back out'. Brown hurried to comply, "I had no sooner started it, when the starboard engine went Voomf! There were flames for about 3-4 seconds and then it went out." The culprit was found to be a cracked component in the fuel system that had subsequently sprayed fuel over the hot engine. There was a happy ending though, "Unbelievably, the deHavilland Canada representative to Vietnam was on the base. He stripped and rebuilt the back of the engine overnight and totally rewired it. The aircraft flew out the next day."

At Vung Tau the Australian Caribous were supported by RAAF ground crews, about whom Brown cannot speak too highly. Unlike the American system of "Crew Chiefs" assigned to a single aircraft and expected to be a 'jack of all trades', the RTFV was supported by a team of skilled RAAF tradesmen. "An aircraft would come in unserviceable and 10 people would hit it. Bang. The next morning it was on the flight-line, ready to go. It was a 24 hour-a-day job and they worked like drovers' dogs." On arriving in Vietnam in 1965, Brown's tour of duty was originally six months, though this was extended to eight months whilst he was there. In that entire time he can only recall three or four occasions when a full complement of aircraft was not at the ready.

When describing the suitability of the Caribou to its role, he puts it simply, "100 per cent. It was a lovely aeroplane and very strong." Warmly describing it as a "truck with wings", he states that he never had cause to shut down an engine in flight and rarely was an engine change required for anything other than reaching its scheduled 'life'. Coupled with its amazing short field performance, its sturdy reliability has seen the Caribou serve in numerous theatres of operation since Vietnam. For Brown, his 'tour' ended in January of 1966 and he subsequently entered the civil ranks of QANTAS. Now in retirement, he was present at a recent air show when the air, dust and crowd were stirred up by the distinctive growl of the deHavilland Caribou. For those in attendance it was a display of impressive low level manoeuvrability and short field performance. For Barrie Brown it probably evoked memories of the mountains of Vietnam, tight airstrips, old friends and the occasional flying pig.

*****

17

The Little Things

In 1994 I was a very junior First Officer in the process of completing line training with the now 'late' Ansett Australia airlines. To my left sat one of Ansett's most experienced training Captain's on the 737 who had been on the type since the earlier -200 model had been introduced. I was to be the pilot flying on the sector, a simple hop from Melbourne to Adelaide with clear skies and fair winds, ideal for a 'bog rat' like myself attempting to master my first jet transport aeroplane.

Cleared for take-off on runway 27 I pressed the TOGA buttons to bring the aircraft to life. The autothrottles promptly advanced, hunted a moment for the correct N1 and then held steady. Through "80 knots", "V1" and "Rotate", the 737-300 eased into the sky with a minimum of effort. I called for gear up and seemingly no sooner than the undercarriage had nestled into their respective wheel wells, when we heard a 'thump'. Wonderfully indistinctive, the sound was significant enough to be met with a mutual and instantaneous turn of our heads. This was followed by one of those dreaded flight deck phrases, "What was that?" We continued to be focused on the safe climb out of the aeroplane and Mike scanned the dials for any sign of trouble. There only seemed to be one slight 'anomaly'.

Sitting at the bottom of the engine instrument stack sat a pair of vibration gauges. The right hand gauge spoke on behalf of the No. 2 engine and was flickering around a reading of '2' units. Per our checklists, no action was required until a reading of '4' was evident and all other engine indications were normal. We were all aware, and wary, of information provided solely on the basis of vibration gauges. They had been integral in the loss of a 737-400 at Kegworth in England five years earlier when an engine failure had been misidentified and the incorrect engine shut down. The vibration gauge only indicates a level of vibration in the fan, or front section of the engine so as I flew the aircraft, Mike set about further investigation. He delved into the touch screen on the centre console known as the ACARS (Aircraft Communication and Reporting System) to reveal further details of the engine's operation. Within the ACARS, the various stages of the engine revealed their individual levels of vibration and again, nothing stood out as abnormal. As reflected by the gauge, there was only a very slightly elevated level of vibration on the fan of the No. 2 engine. We discussed the option of returning to Melbourne but there was no justifiable reason to do so.

As we topped out in the climb and rolled over into level flight, the thrust levers retarded to the cruise setting and all evidence of the vibration disappeared. The vibration gauge now read zero. With all seemingly back to normal, we reviewed the event and had another look at the ACARS; still nothing of consequence. We spoke by radio to our engineers and they had nothing further to offer. On such a short sector we continued to manage the flight and pay attention to the housekeeping duties as the marker for top of descent steadily rolled down the navigation display in front of me. As we pitched into descent and idle thrust was set, we scanned the engine instruments again. Nothing. Zero. Zilch. Operations normal. I decided to delay my head scratching and concentrate on the descent profile for Runway 05 at Adelaide which called for a crossing of the coast at Port Stanvac and, hopefully, a smooth decelerating arc over the water to intercept final approach. At that time, Ansett procedures had a minimum 'spool up' height of 800' AGL. In essence, the most efficient descent saw the Boeing glide with the thrust levers at idle until the final stage of approach when, by 800', the thrust levers were set for power on approach. On this sector my training was bearing fruit and the descent went very close to plan.

On final approach, wings level, configured and coming through about 1200' I 'clicked out' the autothrottle and manually eased the thrust levers up to an appropriate power setting. At about this time it felt like someone had started taking to the aircraft with a sledge hammer. The No. 2 vibration flicked full circle and seemed to bounce off the stops. In a blink, Mike called "taking over" and began to retard the right hand thrust lever back with some resultant relief. The runway loomed large, too late for checklists and a go-around seemed far from prudent. We entered the flare and Mike smoothly closed the thrust levers. The shudder was gone and we touched down right on the money as the Captain pulled asymmetric reverse thrust, not wanting to risk the starboard engine. Clear of the runway, all indications were again normal, though we taxied to the terminal without raising the No.2 engine above idle, just in case.

We parked at the terminal and completed our shutdown checklists. The ground engineer plugged in his headsets with the accompanying eardrum rupturing 'squawk'. Before we had an opportunity to say a word he opened up with, "You gotta see this." The comment somewhat heightened our interest. After the passengers had disembarked we followed suit and made our way to the starboard engine nacelle. There was blood on the lip of the nacelle indicating a bird-strike, but further in a number of the engine's fan blades were badly bent. Three of them through almost 90 degrees so that they were pointing forward instead of running around the inner wall of the cowling. There was further biological evidence of the demise of a feathered being that, fortunately for us, had passed through the fan blades of the high-bypass engine but totally missed the engine's core. This bird had been the 'thump' we had heard shortly after take-off out of Melbourne.

Airframe and engine vibrations on board aircraft can be very difficult to diagnose. Their severity is often a combination of such things as airspeed, airflow angle, power settings, and the like. In the event of such vibration, many checklists call for a change in altitude, attitude and airspeed as a possible remedy. In our case, the landing configuration and body angle provided the correct mix for the vibration to fully manifest. However, seeing the resultant damage also reflects the durability of modern jet engines.

Perhaps one of the most valuable lessons that day lay in the nature of the engine problems. Prior to entering the airline world I had spent much of my time training pilots in engine failures of all descriptions. Single engine practise forced landings, engine failures after take-off (EFATO) and asymmetric flight in all phases and corners of the envelope. The 737 conversion continued its engine failure emphasis with V1 cuts, engine fires, turbine seizures, failures in the cruise and so on. Almost exclusively, there was a distinct loss of power with resultant yaw. This was then followed by textbook procedures, resulting in a textbook outcome. The real world does not always throw up the standard scenario. It may be a partial loss of power, totally contradictory engine indications or a combination of conflicting symptoms. Whatever the case, the first priority is always to fly the aeroplane. Don't rush in, take a breath and attempt to gather as much information as possible and then manage the situation. Many critical errors have been made in haste.

Until the final stage of the approach on our short journey from Melbourne to Adelaide, all we effectively experienced was a 'bump' and an 'in tolerance' vibration indication that subsequently disappeared. To see the fan blades of that starboard engine I would have expected far greater drama. We are all trained for when things go terribly wrong. We have drills, procedures and checklists in place to keep the most injured aeroplane aloft. Unfortunately reality doesn't always fall within the guidelines of a syllabus. Be it the crippled DC10 at Sioux City or the more subtle confusion of Kegworth, neither were a 'standard' training scenario prior to the event. Certainly, on occasions emergencies are easily read and then again, sometimes it's the little things.

*****

18

Fortunate Skies

When I returned from 'There and Back', my around Australia flight to raise funds for the Royal Flying Doctor Service, I had time to reflect upon a vast array of memories from different perspectives. Having traversed the length and breadth of the country and conducted countless interviews and speaking engagements, certain questions continued to surface. These questions bolster my belief that most folks don't have an appreciation of what aviation is really about. Unfortunately, many of these enquiries came from educated individuals reporting for the media. These same individuals will be called to report about aviation again at some point, be it an incident or community outrage at a nearby airport. We can only hope for an accurate and level account when the time comes.

By far one of the most common and telling questions was, "Don't you get bored up there?" Now picture this, you're hand flying a light aircraft on a trek of 13,000km. Between waypoints, there can be quite some distance, so managing the aeroplane, its fuel flow and navigating amongst pockets of weather most certainly accounts for some time and that answer was met by journalists with understanding nods. However, how do you describe the awe-inspiring vantage point of flight at around 5,000 feet to a layman? It is a height that is significant enough to offer a wonderfully detailed panorama of the land below, but not so great that the detail fades to grey.

This realm is home to the majority of visual pilots, yet to place another metaphorically into the pilot's seat with justice calls for a mastery of the language that few possess. It is much like describing art and the fact that beauty is in the eye of the beholder. Yet inevitably we all try to and are generally met by a blank expression, although occasionally a twinkle of interest creeps into the corner of their eye.

At the other end of the spectrum were those fellow aviators who came out to see my trusty aeroplane and discuss the machine and the mission. Rather than looking at these people, I was more commonly looking in the same direction; at some detail of the aircraft or to the sky above, assessing the weather. The base-line was a common interest in flight and with that established, the conversation flowed freely.

Aloft once more (and not bored at all), the contrast gave me cause for thought about a simple truth. We are so fortunate in this day and age to be able to take to the skies, either in a two seat monoplane, or at Mach 0.86 and Flight Level 370. My flight celebrated the centenary of powered flight in Australia and there is no denying the incredible advancement of aerospace technology in that time. Equally impressive is the accessibility of aviation.

In the early days, aviators were lauded as heroes, both incredibly brave and perhaps a little mad. Regardless, of their motivating traits, they were undisputed pioneers forging a new frontier, not just on foreign soil, but in a new dimension. There were no guarantees of success, or even of personal safety. Reliability was not a consideration as most undertakings were sought to be conquered just once. A warring world and brilliant minds saw the novelty of aviation transform from its fledgling hops to a reliable means of global transport in less than the span of a human life. Few other human endeavours can lay claim to such progress.

Today, flight is truly feasible. I have often said that the most remarkable aspect of flying around Australia was that it was relatively unremarkable. In 1928, Bert Hinkler flew solo from England to Australia in 15 days with his head in the breeze and an atlas on his lap. For my part I had an enclosed cockpit, starter motor, VHF radio, emergency beacon, satellite tracking system, GPS, accurate charts, mobile phone coverage and so on. When Hinkler was lost on the Tuscan Mountains it took months for him to be found and then it was only a fluke. I may have run slightly late for dinner had I been forced down in a remote area.

And yet, a forced landing is also a relatively rare occurrence in the modern day. Today, reliability is a major consideration and technology has evolved to make that an accepted reality. Armed with a modern aircraft, competent training and sound preparation, an 'adventure' like mine is within most pilots reach. Burning around 23 litres per hour to attain over 200 km/h is good economy and a great distance can be covered in a day at that pace.

We live in an age of accessible aviation and we should probably stop and digest that from time to time. There are obstacles, no doubt. The encroachment of the metropolis upon airfields, the uncertain future of some aviation fuels and the hurdles associated with modern security measures. Notwithstanding, it is still far easier to capture a slice of sky than could ever have been imagined a century ago. In fact in 1928, Hinkler was bold enough to suggest that, "one day, people will fly by night and use the daylight for sightseeing." And he was considered an advanced thinker on the topic.

Rather than getting caught up in the frustrations that can limit our enjoyment at times, let's appreciate the unique experience we share. Stop and smell those roses in the clouds. What we do when our wheels leave the earth is very special, but not out of the reach of the masses. Many people have just never had the opportunity, or possess a phobia that could easily be dispelled with a little knowledge. Maybe that is something we should all undertake to do more often and win over some of the 'nay-sayers'

Flight has transformed our planet, but it has also offered a view of our earth as we could only once have imagined. We are indeed fortunate that our passion for the skies and our birth dates placed us here in the right time and place. We should all enjoy aviation and celebrate the freedom it offers. And in case you're still wondering, no, I never get bored up there.

*****

19

We Lead, Others Follow

For those who have seen the BBC's production, "Bomber Crew" it provided a great insight into the torrid nature of the war in the night skies over Europe. Beyond the footage of heavily laden Lancasters clawing into the air, hunting searchlights and devastation on the ground is a significant undercurrent; one of youth. These were very young men undertaking a very deadly task. From within their ranks came an elite group that in the dark of night led the way and marked the targets; these were the Pathfinders.

Today, Selwyn Booth sits quietly across from me; mild-mannered, well-dressed and precise in his choice of words. Years may well weary them, but like many of these aging veterans, Selwyn has a bearing that reflects the pride and determination of a well-spent youth. The memory is clear, the eyes still sharp and at times the corner of the mouth curls up into the grin of the young navigator who was awarded the Distinguished Flying Cross.

He hailed from Kempsey on the NSW north coast where dairy

farming, not air raids, were the norm. Answering the call in June of 1942, Selwyn was put through the hoops of recruit training in Australia before embarking for Canada in April 1943 where he was to learn his trade under the banner of the Empire Air Training Scheme. The first five month's abroad were spent with No. 8 Bomb and Gunnery School at Lethbridge and then onto Edmonton for Air Observer's School. Completing his training as an Air Bomber in October, Selwyn could now dispense with the tell-tale white hat band designating a trainee and proudly wear the "O" half-wing brevet of qualified aircrew. By month's end he had landed in England where any number of postings was in the offing, with the air war over Europe in full swing and losses mounting as a consequence.

RAF Bomber Command was predominantly involved in night bombing operations in an attempt to reduce the staggering losses of daylight raids. This strategy was at the cost of precision as locating and then hitting the target in darkness became a distinct challenge. In fact, roughly only a quarter of bombs were "on target", which by definition was within three miles of the aiming point. In 1942, necessity once again mothered invention and the concept of the Pathfinders was put forward. This involved the creation of a select force whose task was to locate and mark the proposed targets with flares in advance of the main bomber fleet. It called for a higher degree of navigational training and the equipping of Pathfinder aircraft with the latest technology to aid in their challenging task. At first the idea was resisted by the head of Bomber Command, Air Vice Marshall Arthur "Bomber" Harris, as he feared the creation of an 'elite' unit would have an adverse impact upon the morale of the majority of bomber crews. Despite his reservations, the Pathfinders were created and in command was an Australian, Group Captain

Donald Bennett of Toowoomba. A pre-war officer, Bennett had established a reputation with a series of long distance flights in flying boats and the establishment of the Atlantic Ferry organisation that eventually saw the delivery of thousands of aircraft. By virtue of this, Bennett had a keen interest and superior skill in the area of aerial navigation, thus making him a prime candidate for the newly created posting.

Pathfinders proudly wore the distinguishing badge of an eagle on the flap of their left breast pocket. A prized insignia, Selwyn admits, "I don't think I ever knew what qualified you to wear the badge. I know it wasn't issued straight away and you had to fly operationally before receiving it." Whereas a normal Bomber Command tour consisted of thirty operations, the Pathfinders' tour totalled forty five so as to gain the maximum return on the specialised training and the crews' experience in marking targets. Marking targets in turn was broken down into responsibilities within the Pathfinders. 'Finders' located the target and marked it initially before 'Illuminators' dropped flares to light up the aiming point. 'Backers-Up' kept the aim point bright by dropping additional flares. All the while an experienced 'Master Bomber' would circle overhead and co-ordinate the attack.

For Selwyn Booth, the trip across the Atlantic had seen his introduction to the heavier bombers in the form of the Handley Page Halifax. Whilst the opportunity to become a Pathfinder was one to be sought after, selection was fundamentally beyond the individual's control. "The pilot chose his crew. He had been selected for the Pathfinder Force and then set about picking who he wanted." Selwyn explained. "Our pilot, Colin Ottaway, was from Perth, our Tail-Gunner Gordon Cornett and Navigator II Allan Brown were from

Sydney and the Wireless Air-Gunner, Wally Blackburn was from Melbourne. The Upper-Gunner and Engineer were both English." Though geographically widespread in their origins, the crew pulled together well and as Selwyn reflects, "We were very compatible". Due to the higher navigational demands and standards, Pathfinders carried two navigators. Working in tandem, the Navigator II would take sightings and using his H2S, Loran or Gee system determine the aircraft's position. This information would be relayed to the Navigator I who would subsequently plot the track and relay the information to the pilot.

In July 1944 Selwyn was placed with No. 1652 Heavy Conversion Unit at RAF Marston Moor. Here he flew with Ottaway as his pilot mastered the Halifax and then set about an Air-to-Sea firing exercise. In September the crew moved to the Pathfinder Navigation Training Unit at Warboys, Hunts where they were introduced to their new aircraft, the legendary Avro Lancaster. Selwyn can't speak highly enough of the bomber that saw him through his operational tour and described its suitability to the demanding task simply as "110%". The following month it was onto Downham Market in Norfolk and posting to their new unit; 635 Squadron, Pathfinder Force (PFF). The squadron motto, "Nos ducimus ceteri secunter", quite fittingly means, "We lead, others follow". Selwyn's first familiarisation flight on October 9th was with the Commanding Officer at the helm, Wing Commander S. "Tubby" Baker DSO and Bar, DFC and Bar. Baker would remain CO until March the following year at which time he had completed a daunting 100 operational sorties.

Downham Market was one of the numerous launching pads from which, night after night, armadas of Stirlings, Mosquitoes and

Lancasters launched into the black oblivion. Laden with men and munitions, they would hold their course in the face of daunting odds and menacing searchlights to deliver their bomb load to the very heart of the Third Reich. On missions that could typically last in excess of eight hours, the crew had only their layered clothing and leather helmets to protect them from the blizzard of high altitude and the deafening drone of the roaring engines. Yet this is exactly what these young men did and at a very high rate of attrition in terms of men and machines. From Downham Market alone, 160 aircraft and around 900 lives were lost on operations.

In the face of statistics and the law of probability, Selwyn and his crew survived 43 missions as Pathfinders. With a wry smile and still an air of disbelief, he rates his escape on only the crew's second mission as probably their luckiest. On the night of 23rd October 1944, Lancaster "M for Mike" with Selwyn and his crew was holding overhead at Downham Market having survived a raid on Essen. The Engineer, like the rest of his crew, was new at his task and it is suspected that he experienced some 'finger trouble' in managing the fuel selection. As a consequence, two engines failed and the Lanc was left to make a two-engine approach at night. Things then further went awry after touchdown as the Lancaster overshot the field and ploughed through an adjacent paddock, collecting two 18,000 Volt transformers and the associated power lines. Breaking its back in the process, the Lancaster came to rest and the uninjured crew evacuated with due haste and scampered clear of the crippled bomber. Crippled but still potent, as Selwyn adds, "We also had a 500lb bomb hung up at the time." Two engines out, a crash landing, high voltage power lines and live ordinance; all on their second mission.

Whilst not all missions ended with such drama, the pre-flight routine was fairly standard and being in the Pathfinders did have some advantages as Selwyn relates, "We generally got the good equipment and the good food". If you weren't involved in a daylight operation, you would spend the morning on standby before a briefing at 1430 hours. Take-off would be planned for around 1830, which would see the crews returning in the wee hours of the morning before undergoing an intelligence de-briefing. This was also accompanied by a greatly appreciated meal, regardless of the hour.

Amongst the collection of items Selwyn has in his possession, a chart catches my attention. It is in remarkably good condition and details a mission to Worms on Germany's Rhine River on a night in February 1945. The crew's 27th operation, the chart portrays mission planning that is matched by diligence in execution. A meticulous log shadows the green pencil line enroute to the target, every three minutes the actual position is logged against the planned route, which seems to be bound for Strasbourg. Then, on the last leg inbound, the track line jinks northward towards Worms in an apparent act of deception to keep the Luftwaffe guessing. Selwyn informs me that such tactics were common, in fact the bombers on occasions crossed the Channel to the North and proceeded over Holland before spearing off to the south. At the target a time, accurate to a fraction of a minute, is boldly boxed on the old chart and then the track turns to red and points home to England; the accurate plotting continues. A notation of "H2S goes U/S", identifies that the ground-looking navigation system (H2S) has failed and won't be of further use on the way home.

On cross-checking the chart with Selwyn's immaculately maintained log-book, a simple notation, "Good Marking" is the only comment.

The log is full of such concise recollections of daytime missions, written in green, and night operations, inked in red; "12 Holes", "Many Fighters", "Good Attack", "Returned on 3 Engines", "Heavy Flak" and "Very Heavy Flak". The intensity of the conflict is in no way eroded by the economy of words; it is impact by understatement. Further detail is forthcoming when I delve verbally, though again one is met with a refreshing degree of modesty. The tenth sortie to Duisburg and its comments about Messerschmitt Bf109s gains my attention. Selwyn recounts, "We were attacked by 109s. There were three attacks and the pilot manoeuvred vigorously to escape the fighters. Seated at our Navigators table, we could feel the positive and negative 'G' forces and watched our parachutes alternately float and fall nearby. We lost about 10,000 feet before we were free of the fighters and flew home on three engines." On their return, the aircraft was found to have collected ten noteworthy holes for their efforts. Such attention from the fighters often followed being picked up in the beams of the German searchlights. In particular "crossed beams", where the lumbering bombers were trapped in the gaze of a number of beams. Flak was another great threat to the raiding bombers. "The Ruhr was heavily defended and consequently there was heavy flak there." Selwyn recalls. On one operation, with flak bursting around them, a fragment pierced the Lancaster and flashed past his fellow Navigator's face, nicking the switch on his oxygen mask. "A couple of inches either way and he would have caught it". Selwyn adds.

In March of 1945, three log-book entries stand out. Firstly, because they are daylight raids on Cologne, Essen and Dortmund. Secondly, they bear the notation, "1,000 bombers". These were the famous raids in conjunction with the Americans where one thousand bombers filled the skies. Selwyn remembers that forming up was one of the greatest challenges, not to mention that there was "no love lost between the Americans and the RAF. The Americans had better uniforms and pay than us and I never met one that didn't remind us of the fact." Once the bombers had rendezvoused, they flew with only 500 feet vertical separation which led to some unfortunate instances where bombs were dropped on their own aircraft.

In the midst of such horrendous warfare, there were lighter moments which reinstate Selwyn's smile. "On one occasion we were told we were not going; we were stood down. So our crew then proceeded to have a few drinks at the bar when someone changed their mind and told us to go." With the tone of a nineteen year old, Selwyn admits that the oxygen was used to offset the effects of a couple of beers on this occasion. Another time, venturing out from their Nissen Hut accommodation and the pot-belly stove, the crew visited London and was caught up in a German V1 flying-bomb attack. "We had heard V2s go over on occasions, but this V1 hit London, not far from us." Naturally curious, Selwyn and Co. went to inspect the scene and "Very nearly got arrested."

The RAF's last bombing sortie of World War Two was flown from Downham Market on the night of 2nd May 1945. Selwyn was not a part of it with his crew having flown their 43rd and final sortie on April 18th, a 1,000 bomber raid over Heligoland. A number of subsequent trips were flown as a "Blighty Express", returning prisoners-of-war to England. By September, with the war over, Selwyn was on his way home to Australia after 2 ½ years abroad. One last order of business before he embarked involved the award of the Distinguished Flying Cross (DFC). The Citation reads;

"PILOT OFFICER BOOTH has completed numerous missions

against the enemy, in the course of which he has invariably displayed the utmost fortitude, courage and devotion to duty."

Rather than rest on his laurels, Selwyn is VERY quick to point out that both he and his pilot, FLTLT Ottaway, received the DFC, yet none of the other crew did. He states simply, "We were commissioned officers and the rest of the crew wasn't and they didn't receive the non-commissioned equivalent, the Distinguished Flying Medal." He laments that the rest of the crew took all of the same risks and contributed equally to their success, yet only the officers received the awards. Again, modesty and humility is very evident.

In the 1980s, Selwyn travelled to Europe and visited Germany at sea level. He was struck by the Church Tower at Cologne which had survived the bombings, just as St. Pauls had remained in spite of the blitz on London. On the same trip he ventured out to Downham Market and the remnants of the once vital cog in RAF Bomber Command's machine. Some Nissen Huts remained as did the Church and a memorial to the Pathfinders, however the airstrip from which he had operated was now overgrown. As with many veterans of conflict, reflection is very often stated with the simplest recollections. For Selwyn the breakfast table at the Mess was the scene of so many faces; faces that may not be there tomorrow. Or spaces at that same table the next morning for reasons that no-one need state. When squadron losses are quoted, Selwyn applies human arithmetic, "That's seven dead per aeroplane." Sixty years on, the significance of what was achieved and what was lost has not faded. To those, like Selwyn, for whom history is not a textbook but the experience of their youth such recollections are very real. They are not second hand facts. They were Pathfinders, an elite unit in Harris' Bomber Command, but most of all they were young men. Seven young men per aeroplane.

*****

20

So You Want to be a Pilot?

I recently took a young lad for a flight over our local district; just a hop for half an hour or so. He keenly looked down upon the earth with that bright-eyed enthusiasm that all youngsters with dreams of flight in their hearts tend to do. For me, it's over forty years since my father shared that experience with me for the first time, although I still vividly remember the ground falling away from the Cessna's wheel outside my window. It was liberating and to quote John Gillespie Magee's immortal poem 'High Flight', I truly felt that we had "slipped the surly bonds of Earth". The fuse had been lit and the fire was to rage inside me until my turn came to take my own aircraft aloft.

Along the way the journey would prove to be both a struggle and an adventure. There would be weeks where the wage only just covered the rent but there would be nights where the sounds of the New Guinea jungle would play an amazing tune as I hung in my hammock. There would be life in a caravan in the midst of 40 degree heat and nights where the ice was getting so thick on the wings that I was sure there was no way out. I would bury good friends who had fallen in harm's way and bury relationships that couldn't overcome the distance and absence. But at the end of the day, I was flying.

Aviation was much more than a career choice for me; it was more akin to feeding an addiction. I had never possessed an alternative 'life plan' and always figured that I'd never need one. Yet now as I contemplate aviation on another 3am drive to the airport, I question whether it is everything thing to me that it once was. Had the dream become little more than a means to an end? For so much has changed in the industry that it is almost unrecognisable when compared to that first flight in that tiny, gleaming Cessna.

The face of the pilot has been through many transformations over the last century. From fledgling pioneers to heroic knights of the air, the aviators were seen as keen, strong and fearless. And in those days they definitely needed to be, although a little dose of 'crazy' was also a useful ingredient in the mix. When the world found the post-war peace of the 1950s and the airliners began to span the globe, it was not so much heroism as glamour that now painted the picture of the pilot. Exotic foreign lands and five-star hotels were the office, while the flight deck laid at his feet views of grand diversity. And they were 'his' feet as the airlines were still a man's domain. Obviously this imbalance needed to change and finally it did when it was realised that women could actually operate airliners just as effectively as their male counterparts. But while this door opening was a change for the better, it was far from the only change.

Jet travel saw the slashing of flight times and crossing the globe moved away from the perception of luxury travel that was more akin to a cruise liner. World travel became big business where deals across borders could be sealed with a handshake in a matter of hours, rather than days. Passengers no longer had to layover in exotic ports, but could catch connecting flights and travel through the night to be home days earlier. And while these changes offered up a variety of worthwhile options for the customer, the role of the airline pilot was beginning to change.

And change it did. No longer did the role resemble the ship's captain surveying the world from the bridge; instead the pilot became more closely related to the hard-working truck driver. Additionally, the security needs of a fragile world meant that air-crews were faceless creatures secured away in a bullet-proof flight deck. Like a rare species of nocturnal mammal, a glimpse of them could be caught if you happened to be in just the right place at the right time. The children's visits to the flight deck were now a thing of the past and announcements about the world passing outside the windows were replaced by in-seat entertainment and iPads.

As fuel prices rose and fiscal reality rammed home, the five-star stop-overs disappeared. Low-cost carriers emerged to place further pressure on the bottom line of an already capital-intensive industry. In some quarters, pilots began to pay for their own training to effectively buy a 'jet job' and their wages dropped as well. Fiscal reality had arrived for aviation and its survival depended on squeezing every inch of efficiency out of the operation in what was now a highly competitive industry. Multiple days of sight-seeing in foreign ports disappeared and 'turn-arounds' became minimal before it was time to turn around and cross back over some great ocean or continent once again. Travel became more routine and frequent and over a far greater distance and time. Sleep became the really valuable commodity to the pilots and crews flying to Europe could routinely feel their 'body clock' passing them in the opposite direction somewhere over Afghanistan. Days off at home would be spent re-adapting to the time-zone just in time to leave again. Similarly, domestic flying became a series of multi-sector days, with minimum rest at the hotel before the transport would be shuttling the crew back to the airport for another day in the saddle. Just as glamour had replaced heroism, routine and efficiency had become the pilot's new benchmark.

It was still dark as I now pulled into the airport car park to start another day. I spared a thought for the young lad with the gleam in his eye and a burning desire to fly. I contemplated my own career and wondered if I had foreseen the hours of study, the cost of training and the years of minimum wage and second jobs would I have been so enthusiastic? If I had foreseen the freezing cold pre-dawn pre-flight inspections and the lonely hours waiting for passengers at hot remote airstrips, would I have accepted the challenge? If someone had told me that the airline operations would become just like any other job, would I have listened to them? If I had known then all that I know now, would I have ever chosen to be a pilot?

Yes.

Absolutely. In a heart-beat.

*****

Seven young men. Selwyn Booth (3rd from left) and his Pathfinder crew. (Photo: S. Booth)

Wallaby Airlines. A Royal Australian Air Force Caribou in Vietnam. (Photo: Barrie Brown)

21

A Classic Morning

The phone vibrates on the table beside the bed, but to be honest I was already half awake. I have been getting up in the early hours to go flying for more years than I have been driving a car. At first it was to steal a ride beside my father, now it is to sit at the front of my own aircraft. Back then there was no subtle alarm to wake me, if I was fortunate my mother would call my name through a crack in the door, but more likely it was my Dad. His less than subtle voice would accompany the bedroom light switching on and the sheets being ripped back from my cocooned form; "Come on boy!"

Today I reach across, silence the alarm and calculate the minutes to the hotel's pre-arranged wake-up call. It's a good start as I immediately know which city I'm in and my orientation is underway. This is not always the case and sometimes it takes a moment or two to assess the location of the TV's red standby lamp and the streetlight's glow creeping around the curtain's edge to get my bearings.

I know that it's a frosty Canberra morning outside and I throw my legs over the side of the bed in one action that takes me beyond the point of no return. Through the night, the cold has obviously infiltrated the concrete and now it greets my bare feet through the carpet. I just can't wait for icy touch of the tiled bathroom floor! I metaphorically smack myself over the back of the head at being so precious. I've lived in caravans and literally slept under the wing; these days I have a hotel room and a car that takes me to the airport. Toughen up Princess!

Showered and shaved, everything is in its place from the night before. My bag is packed and the ironed uniform hangs in the wardrobe. I flick the kettle on and sit down to review the latest weather on my iPad to give me a 'heads up' for the day ahead. The cup of tea hardly touches the sides and I zip up my gear and turn off the light switch before going to 'Reception' and receiving the dreaded question, "Your room number?" I know which city I'm in and wonder why I'm the only one in the foyer satisfied with that depth of knowledge.

One by one the crew filter downstairs and greetings are mixed with complaints, conversation and the shuffling of the daily newspaper. All as one we move outside where the frozen morning smacks us in the face like a burst from an icy garden hose. Bags in the back of the van, we take our seats and move off as the personal introductions continue. However, the internal light of the mini-bus remains off and a few of the crew grab those last cherished moments of sleep.

At the airport, we move up the escalators and onto security where there are very few passengers, but delivery men having their newspapers and various goods scanned by the X-Ray. We split from the cabin crew and proceed to briefing where synoptic charts, NOTAMs, flight plans and a state-of-the-art coffee machine greet us.

As usual, a chance of fog is forecast at Canberra just before the sun decides to arrive, but otherwise the dominant high pressure system over central Australia is providing fine weather across the nation. If we can escape Canberra without delay, it's shaping to be a good day. We order the fuel and the ground staff let us know that our aircraft is parked on a stand-off bay without an aerobridge, so it'll be a brisk walk to the aeroplane.

Leaving the warmth of the terminal, I head up the stairs as my partner in this venture walks around the outside and casts a particularly careful eye over the airframe for frost or ice. There is no fog at this stage, but Jack Frost can still visit the skin of the Boeing 737-400, or 'Classic', that we have been tasked to fly.

Up the stairs and into the flight deck, I walk into the darkened workspace that has not received its wake-up call. Bringing a cold aircraft to life always reminds me of the scene from Tom Hank's Apollo 13 movie, where they crawl back into the lunar module that they'd previously shut down. A maze of switches and circuit breakers, frozen from the night before as my torchlight skips around the panels before a safety check and the battery switch brings the aircraft partially back to life.

There's fire warnings and circuit breakers to check before the Auxiliary Power Unit in the tail-cone is brought online. As I turn the switch to do so I can hear the click of relays and watch the flick of gauges as the load on the battery increases. And then the low rumble and slow whistle moves up the aisle from the tail to reassure me that the start cycle is truly underway. It's a characteristic of smaller jets on quiet mornings that I've grown to appreciate, for once the APU has come to life the aircraft has a pulse and a minute later, respiration to breathe warm air into the cabin. I carry out some further checks and ensure the galley power and coffee brewers are on their way before I settle into the 'piloting stuff'.

Align the navigation system, scan the flight deck panels, check the oxygen system, set the radios and program the Flight Management Computer and so on. The list seems endless, but after twenty years and two airlines I'm getting the hang of it. The cabin crew now shuffles up the stairs and my partner is back from the walk around where some frost was sighted on the airframe. I cast a glance over my shoulder and the rugged up engineer is already aloft in the 'cherry picker' and spraying de-icing fluid on the wing. I grab out another manual as the spraying of this fluid calls for extra procedures and a little more time, but still there is no fog.

Over the next fifteen minutes the performance for the aircraft is calculated with due respect for the variable winds, de-icing procedure and hill off the end of the runway. The magic of the electronic flight bag provides us with the answers after we independently input the data and cross-check our findings. It's still dark as the passengers cross the tarmac in their coats, gloves and hats, while the air traffic controllers have only just brought their control tower back on line. We verify the latest weather at the airfield against our calculations and trouble the controller to read back our airways clearance.

It's T minus ten minutes and we brief our departure and various scenarios before running a checklist. The log books and fuel docket rest outside against the window in a box on the end of a pole designed specifically for the task. The documentation is checked and the refuelling numbers are calculated and verified. As the last passengers are taking their seats, the final load sheet with its weights, stabiliser trim setting and persons on board is messaged to the aeroplane where the figures are again cross checked and entered into the FMC. We pressurise the hydraulic system, check the flight controls, hand out the last of the paperwork to the cabin manager, shut the door, and complete the final checklist. It's T minus two minutes, let's go.

The engineer assures us that the airframe is clear of frost through our headsets before we ask for pushback clearance, release the brakes and start the engines. The oil pressure already sits quite high as the cold viscous oil pushes through the system awaiting the warmth of combustion elsewhere in the engine. With both engines started and providing electrical power, the APU is shutdown and the brakes are set. The tractor and engineer disconnect and the latter waves us goodbye. There are a few final precautions against icing to conduct before yet another checklist, request for taxi clearance and we're underway to the accompaniment of the safety demonstration in the background.

We bump along the taxiway initially as the bottoms of the tyres have a frozen flat spot from sitting at below zero temperatures through the night. As they roll along the taxiway, the rubber warms and as the round shape returns, the subtle thumping dissipates. Our red anti-collision beacon has a stroboscopic effect on the scenery around us and still there is no evidence of fog except for the odd wisp around lights on the corners of nearby hangars. The chimes sound on the flight deck to let us know that the cabin is secure and ready for departure just as the clock confirms that the five minute engine warm up period has passed. The final checklist is completed to verify flap and stabiliser settings before we call the tower and let them know we're ready for take-off. With no other aircraft on frequency and none sighted on approach to land, we're cleared for take-off and line up at the end of Runway 35.

Our flashing strobe lights and landing light beams are droll by comparison to the runway lighting ahead. A mix of colours and lines of light illuminate the black strip of asphalt. The thrust levers are brought forward and the engine noise spools up, slowly pushing the aircraft from its stationary pose. The TOGA button is pressed and the thrust levers move further forward to the take-off setting, now driven by their own servo motors as the Boeing gathers genuine momentum.

"80 knots." The runway lights flash past.

"V1." The hand leaves the thrust levers.

"Rotate." The runway lights disappear beneath the nose.

Another day is underway. I love my job.

*****

22

Going Solo

On the 'Author' page of this book is a photograph of a small lad peering over the cockpit's edge. Leather helmet and goggles still in place, he had just been aloft when his equally excited father snapped this image. For me, it is one of my favourite photos as it captures the collision between the joy of flight and the unharnessed enthusiasm of youth. But there is even more to this picture than a wonderful moment frozen in time, for that small boy now stands well over six feet tall and his world has changed forever.

Yesterday as I sat in an airport lounge waiting for my aeroplane to arrive, my phone buzzed into life and a simple message brought a huge grin to my face. "I've gone solo!" That message came from Alex, the young boy in the front cockpit of that Tiger Moth biplane; only he is not a young boy now. In fact he towers over me and possesses a quiet maturity of someone many years older. He is no longer a young kid with stars in his eyes, but a young man with his sights firmly set on the skies. Yesterday, he took his first major step on a long and exciting journey.

His dream of flight has not been a whim, but a slow-cooking desire in a quiet casing. Yet, despite his ever-present interest in aviation, the dream often seemed to be just too far out of reach as the harsh reality of dollars and cents surfaced to spoil the fun. And still he never gave up. Through university and second jobs his passion for flight simmered until this year he took a huge step and applied for an airline pilot cadet scheme. In fact, he was through the first stage of interviews before Alex even told his parents. His Dad is one of my best friends and knew that for Alex to have started these wheels in motion, it must truly be his dream. Without hesitation his parents supported his aspirations even though he was midway through a law degree. He excitedly brought his Dad up to speed on the whole process, but to say it had come out of 'left field' is probably an understatement.

Now, only a matter of weeks later, Alex has flown an aeroplane solo for the first time. That little kid who listened intently every time I spoke about aeroplanes and jumped in the other seat every time I offered him a flight is now the 'Pilot-in-Command' in his own right. It thrills me. Even more inspiring is what his Dad describes as the "joy in his voice" over the long distance phone line from western New South Wales. The thought that Alex is pursuing his passion as much as following a career path is a sentiment that should inspire every youngster that dreams of flight.

For my part, it takes me back to my first solo on a still morning thirty years ago; the anticipation, the excitement, the realisation of being alone up there and then the absolute 'scream at the top of your lungs' happiness when the propeller stops and you realise that you've actually done it. For that, I thank Alex as he has let this old pilot walk in a set of young shoes again, if only for a moment. And for all pilots, of all levels, that moment is something that will be with them forever. "First Solo" is a flight that will not fade like the ink in the log book as the hours pile up over the decades. It is a point in time where the dream became real and self doubt was left at the runway's edge with a nervous instructor watching his prodigy take to the skies.

To all the pilots, to all the instructors and to all the Mums and Dads, thank you. That 'first solo' is a day that will be there forever, stamped in the mind and the log book in indelible ink. Wherever the road takes you, it can never take that from you. Congratulations Alex. The sky is not the limit, now it's your home.

*****

23

Another Year

The boats are once again gathering on the harbour and stakes are claimed by families on the foreshore; both with the intention of seeing in the New Year from the best vantage point. The sight of fireworks erupting above the Sydney Harbour Bridge has become synonymous with an Aussie farewell to the year now gone and "G'day" to the months that lie ahead.

And yet for me, my New Year's Eve began quite some time ago and my vantage point was well aloft in the rarefied atmosphere. Never one for resolutions bound by a calendar's single day, nor have I ever limited my reflections to one particular evening. This is as much a necessity as a philosophy, as many New Year's have passed my sleeping form and the only countdown is the hours until the alarm clock erupts. Epaulettes, charts and suitcases have been as integral to the dawn of my new year as fireworks and champagne is for the revellers. But I'm not complaining.

Often I have been fortunate enough to see the first rays of sun break the horizon on the newly arrived year. While sore heads have slept below, I have seen the clouds transform from an opaque grey mass to a brilliant apricot blanket, before burning off into a crystal clear blue day. All around are the sights that have captured the heart, soul and imagination throughout the year. But then again, they are there on so many days.

As I scooted across the quilted landscape into Adelaide, I relived so many wonderful memories from my charity flight around Australia. Back then I held a chart in one hand as I steered the trusty Jabiru with the other. Now I looked at the landscape below, laid out like an unfolded map slipping past at 300 knots. Sir Hubert Wilkins homestead, that little hamlet with the silos and the 'hidden' sub-station; they are now all laid out before me.

In Canberra I recalled those frosty mornings and early starts and the spectacular spray of de-icing fluid from the lone, brave soul in the cherry-picker. There were those nights in Darwin where the heart of the thunderstorms flashed with enough charge to run a city's lights and make the best fireworks display look tiny in comparison. The unscheduled overnight in Hobart when I froze on the dockside in the winter rain, patiently waiting for my seafood feast. Yes, it was well worth the wait.

The RAAF Hornets blasting past me at Townsville and rain-drops the size of cars near Cairns reminded me why the far north can be such a special place. From east to west and back again, blues and greens that turned white with froth as waves crashed upon our endless coastline. The Alice and The Rock, where remote is a synonym for beauty and whose colours can change with the transit of the sun or a desert downpour. Perth and her growing skies that keep the mines alive are such a far cry from the remote airstrips I called upon as a younger man.

The home of the Lord of the Rings, Queenstown, New Zealand captures my heart every time we trek down the valley past the Bungy Bridge. Those Hobbits knew what they were doing. There is Melbourne with her hot air balloons at dawn and the ghosts of historic Point Cook air base. Was that a Wirraway getting airborne down there and heading out over Port Phillip Bay? And then there's Sydney, picture postcard in so many ways, but more than anything, it is home.

Every day, not just December 31st, I count my blessings for a life in the stratosphere and every single foot beneath it. I recall the day that Neil Armstrong left the surly bonds of Earth for a final time and I remember those mates who have shared the skies and who now reside in the clouds forever. There have been quite a few over the years, but Alan I'm thinking of you just now. God speed mate.

So many memories and images are etched into the mind's eye and locked into the heart. The pain of another early start or simulator check ride is easily forgotten, over-ridden by the thought of a curving contrail turning towards the setting sun. Another year is nearly over, but it only marks the passing of another day, really no more special than any other. It is not a pivotal day of new beginnings; every day is and every day should be cherished with equal fervour.

Nevertheless, as the final page of the calendar on my desk ticks over it is a small landmark of sorts. There is a moment when I pause and put my cherished memories on hold and allow my thoughts to wander further. Now what lies ahead? What new moments await? Perhaps that is what the fireworks are all about, the excitement of special times yet to be lived and new skies still to be discovered.

Happy New Year.

*****

24

Of Dreams and Metal Detectors

In one of those great moments, I recently took my daughter for her first flight in a light aircraft. Her excitement and sheer joy reminded me of a time 40 years ago when my father had first taken me aloft in a seat that was complemented by a control column instead of a tray table. Yet within the period of my lifetime, the face of aviation security has changed so incredibly that one wonders if the joy is being strangled at the grass roots level of aviation.

My parents told tales of barnstorming pilots landing on local farms and taking folks for their first flight in frail machines with open cockpits. Airfields were far more developed by my childhood, but the ability to interact with 'planes and pilots was still common. Airfields were littered with new Pipers, Cessnas and Beechcraft, while DC-3s and Beavers fired up their radials and the Mustangs in civilian garb roared skyward to tow targets for the military. There was all manner of wings to climb upon and instrument panels to gaze at through hands cupped on Perspex.

As long as you paid due respect to taxiways and people's property, there were basically no restrictions for the budding young aviator. Free to wander and explore, query and question. And those who called the airport their home could not encourage the next generation enough, hoisting them into seats and on occasions taking them for that prized goal; a circuit! A small camera with twelve valued frames of film was standard equipment and the week's wait for developing was almost too long to bear. The entire experience of a visit to the airport was about as good as it could get for a keen youngster.

And then the events of 11th September 2001 took place and forever changed our world and our industry.

Flying internationally in the months following the attacks, security screening was heightened to a level never seen. When Richard Reid attempted to take an aircraft down with explosive shoes only a month later, footwear became the next target. Less than two years later, Heathrow was the scene of a strong military presence when fears of a 'surface to air missile' attack raised their head and I walked through Terminal 4 surrounded by combat ready troops. The scene was not so different in 2006 when the 'liquids and gels' Trans-Atlantic plot was foiled. The postcards of Pan-Am Clippers and bow-tied waiters were long gone, now replaced by the harsh reality of a 21st Century under fire.

These security measures were inevitable, not only to deter those who would attack an aircraft, but to provide some degree of confidence in the industry for those who choose to fly. Undoubtedly there will be further measures in the future as one and all recognise that it is an area of ongoing review where complacency is potentially the attacker's greatest weapon. But how has this brave new world affected the next generation of starry-eyed aviators?

At some airfields, easy access has been replaced towering fences and coded security gates. Benches which once offered unobscured views are cordoned off and security vehicles pause and at times question those peering through fences with a telephoto lens. The accessibility of aviation has disappeared for many youngsters and the sterile airline terminal and a windowless aerobridge is the most that is on offer to many. Is this an environment where dreams and excitement can be nurtured as they once were?

In the face of these hurdles there is definitely still hope for the next wave of budding aviators and engineers, however, a greater degree of responsibility also rests with those of us who have already taken to the skies and can remember the times before the sky went a darker shade. Programs such as the 'Young Eagles' in the United States are growing elsewhere and offer an opportunity for youngsters to go flying in a general aviation aeroplane free of charge through the generosity of volunteers. Youth organisations around the world such as Air Cadets seek to encourage air-mindedness and offer opportunities for their members to get see aviation at a closer range than is normally available.

While these organisations do a tremendous job, the responsibility doesn't end with the group; it stays with the individual. As pilots, instructors, owners and engineers we should take the time to avail opportunities to those young minds that show an interest in our chosen endeavour. It may be in the form of organising a school excursion to your airfield, or attending a careers night; it may be even in the form of taking a bright-eyed future aviator for a lap of the airfield. The reality of our times is that these gestures will be less spontaneous and more the subject of procedures and protocol. Accordingly, that will call for a greater degree of organisation and effort, but it is something we must undertake.

Sure, the internet offers images, videos and glimpses of aviation hardware from around the world, but a computer can never impart the true sounds, smells and air-sense that spinning propellers and popping exhausts bring to life. It is as much about atmosphere as it is imagery.

A failure to encourage those coming through will manifest commercially as a 'pilot shortage', but the shortcoming runs much deeper than that; it is the loss of opportunity. Not all those we encourage will pursue aviation as a career or even pursue it as a hobby, but their exposure to aviation and the magic of flight may just set the wheels of imagination and ambition in motion. That one flight may serve to provide a young mind with an insight into why self-discipline is important or how safety is always a consideration. The lesson may just be as simple as someone taking the time out to show an interest.

The headlines will continue to spread gloom about an industry under threat, but that does not mean that there is no room left for a youngster's dreams. In a world of security fences and metal detectors, we all have the ability to go against the trend and encourage the next generation to share in the joy of flight.

*****

25

If These Walls Could Speak

After 14 hours of extended night, a 747-400 rolls onto final approach at Brisbane Airport on Australia's east coast. Gear down, final flaps and checks complete, the modern monolith readies for its return to earth after what seems an eternity to its 350 passengers. As the wheels smack the 1500' markers, the blue smoke puffs from the tyres and another trans-Pacific epic is over. A mere matter of wingspans away, one can almost hear the contempt of the use of the term 'epic' rising from a landscaped garden and discreet glass-fronted hangar. Within these glazed walls stands a worthy recipient of the terms pioneer and legend. Within these glazed walls stands Sir Charles Kingsford Smith's 'Old Bus', The Southern Cross.

The Fokker Tri-Motor stands proudly, surrounded by artifacts relating to its days of glory. Retired, but not forgotten, its current home salutes the trials and tribulations of its historic past and is a far cry from the weather-lashed reality of its heroic adventures. To view the Southern Cross, up close and personal, is a rare privilege. This is not a replica; this is the actual craft that wrote history. An integral part of aviation

134

heritage from a time before pressurisation and Global Positioning Systems; a time of Don Bradman, Babe Ruth and revolutionary talking movies.

"Southern Cross" is boldly displayed in silver along its navy blue flanks, though this was not always the case. The Fokker FVIIB had originally been owned by Arctic explorer, Sir Hubert Wilkins and suffered through a series of trials in Alaska before coming to grief. In 1928, the airframe was bought by 'Smithy' and his trans-Pacific cohort, Charles Ulm and fitted with three new Wright Whirlwind engines. After a series of proving flights, the name "Southern Cross" was proposed by another of the team, Keith Anderson. Originally, this title was supplemented by a reference to a truck manufacturer, "Faegol Flyer", and "The Spirit of California", though these were removed for the trans-Pacific conquest. Finally, the Australian registration of "VH-USU" would adorn the fuselage in company with its name.

If the bearing of the machine impacts upon the spirit, making one's way to the door on the starboard side is ripe with anticipation. Stooping to gain access through a small door, the interior is now manned by a lone wicker chair and a brass fire extinguisher still hanging at the ready. Here Kansas native Jim Warner would strain against the deafening roar to detect the hint of a radio signal while his fellow countryman Harry Lyon plotted the Southern Cross' course in one of history's great efforts of dead reckoning. Thrashed by weather and incessant vibration, Lyon's sextant was of limited value and he relied on the constants of time, heading and groundspeed. Drift was calculated by throwing powder by day and flares by night into the Pacific below and subsequently flying a constant heading. Such rudimentary techniques safely saw the intrepid aviators cross over 11,000 km of ocean by day and night in three historic legs. The cabin's noisy, draughty environment rendered communication ineffective and left the crew temporarily deaf after shutdown. Messages were exchanged between the cabin and cockpit via a stick with notes pinned to the end. These notes were used to relay both operational information and humorous, uplifting messages between the crew as they set about defying the odds. In later life the cabin of the Southern Cross hosted twelve passengers on scenic flights, or eight in the upmarket role of airline transport. Today the tube and fabric hull holds only memories.

From a pilot's perspective, stepping up into the cockpit is more than tinged with excitement. Beyond the cabin's central fuel tank and through the narrow opening sits scant dials, three throttles and the seats which carried Kingsford Smith and Ulm. Entering the cockpit would pose a challenge to a larger man as one ducks beneath the doorway and weaves between the seats, careful not to take a clumsy handhold on some irreplaceable lever. Finally in position, I gingerly lower myself into the historic left hand seat. The dials sit ahead of me and it is impossible not to sense the past as I take a grip of the control wheel. To the right, Ulm's chair sits vacant and the rustic nature of the rag and tube cockpit is evident. Over the nose, visibility is impinged by the cylinders and exhaust stack of the central radial engine; the same culprit engine that blew its exhaust manifold over the Tasman Sea and sent a renegade part hurtling into the starboard propeller with devastating results.

Further dominating the obscured view from Smithy's seat are the broad wings of the Southern Cross. Painted silver, the thick aerofoil is obviously built for lift and not for speed. Within are housed four fuel tanks that are managed by a Heath-Robinson fuel panel behind the pilot's right shoulder. The ergonomics of this machine only add to the awe of the undertaking. These huge wings served to provide shade for the crew when they found themselves alone in the desolate, heat-soaked Kimberley region of Western Australia in 1929. Having flown in excess of 24 hours since departing Sydney and lost in the remote northwest, Smithy finally put the aircraft down on the mudflats where they would wait twelve days for rescue. The episode came to be known as the "Coffee Royal Affair" after the crew had blended spirits with coffee whilst stranded. Unfounded rumors of a publicity stunt cast aspersions on the integrity of Smithy and Ulm. The drama was further heightened by the loss in central Australia of their friend Keith Anderson and Bill Hitchcock in their Westland Widgeon as they searched for the missing men. Damaged, but undaunted, Smithy would continue on and ultimately be the first man to circumnavigate the globe in the same aeroplane. Even so, the stigma of "Coffee Royal" remained.

Whilst the wings and engines obscure the view to port and starboard, an interesting feature is the absence of glass. Despite a central windscreen, pilots are exposed to the elements, noise and churning airflow through the void adjacent to their shoulders. It almost defies the imagination to conjure the conditions experienced on such pioneering flights. Even so, there were instances when even the relative comfort of the cockpit could not be enjoyed. In May of 1935, when the starboard engine had its propeller shattered over the Tasman Sea, the remaining engines labored to keep the Tri-Motor aloft. Trans-Tasman co-pilot P.G "Bill" Taylor climbed through the absent window to starboard and drained oil from the defunct engine so that the life giving fluid could be transferred to the failing port engine. This transfer was repeated and precious mail dumped before the Australian coastline finally came into view. Right engine shutdown, left engine struggling and the centre engine on the verge of failure, the 'Old Bus' staggered to a three-point landing at Sydney after fifteen hours aloft.

This was to be the last major flight for the Southern Cross. Smithy knew that after 300,000 miles his old bus was approaching its 'use by' date and handed her over to the Royal Australian Air Force later that year.

During World War Two, the aircraft was moved to the nation's capital, Canberra, where it was dismantled for storage and maintained. Though the fabric and rubber components were no longer airworthy, the engines were fully overhauled in 1944. She then passed to the civil Department of Aviation and returned to airworthy status in 1945 for a film about its famous owner. After further storage, her final short flight was in 1947 to a nearby air pageant for the Royal Aero Club.

Her subsequent life consisted of darkened hangars, storage facilities and damage to the tail and mainplane from removalist's vans. She was occasionally cleaned and the airscrews turned over once a week. At one stage the 'Southern Cross' was asked to be removed urgently as it was "using up valuable hangar space".

Finally, in 1958, the Fokker Tri-Motor received its due respect and was fully restored to become the central exhibit at Brisbane's Eagle Farm Airport and relocated to the new airport in 1988. There she stands today in a climate-controlled display facility and maintained under a regular schedule of cleaning, inspection and maintenance.

To encounter the Southern Cross at close quarters is a profound experience for any devotee of aviation history. In our modern disposable society, longevity is a rare commodity. The aircraft is basic, rugged and low on technology, but high on mystique. Within its fabric shell and its elevated cockpit, the atmosphere is tangible. Aviation's tall tales and true seem to seep from every corner of the "Old Bus".

The Southern Cross' extraordinary life is well documented, yet, as I sit at the sharp end of this historic machine and imagine a myriad of frozen, oil spattered moments I can't help but feel that there is still much left unsaid. Memories that now lie on ocean floors with the men who made them. Perhaps it is better this way, but one cannot help but wonder what would be said, if these walls could speak.

****

If These Walls Could Speak. The cockpit of Kingsford-Smith's 'Southern Cross'

Does it get any better than this? A Piper Cub on a summer's afternoon.

26

Higher Stakes

The issues challenging the delivery schedule of modern airliners continues to fill the pages of aviation journals around the world. Aircraft development has a long history of difficult births and failed types. Perhaps Howard Hughes' 'Spruce Goose' is an extreme example, but many of the issues that hobbled the Hughes H-4 Hercules are still being revisited today including materials, cost, and deadlines.

Just as Hughes was looking to break boundaries and be revolutionary in what his aircraft could achieve, the big players of Airbus and Boeing decided to step outside the square in their recent forays. In a battle of philosophies, Airbus went for size with the double-deck A380, while Boeing went down the path of composite materials in pursuit of savings and efficiency with the 787. Today, the A380 is now routinely cruising the airways; however it was not without significant development problems. Commencing with wiring issues, the A380 delivery schedule was also pushed back through a series of major announcements which saw their parent company (EADS) share price dive and the departure of a number of senior executives. Even following its delivery there were issues with the Rolls Royce engines and the emergence of small cracks within its wings.

This is VERY big business and the stakes are enormously high. Even to giants of industry like Airbus and Boeing, the costs are astronomic and for that reason various components and contracts are outsourced to share the pain. The days of a production line starting with a bare frame and punching out a completed Flying Fortress at the far end of the building are gone. This is a matter of international logistics and project management and all the communication and co-ordination problems that inevitably come with it.

History has shown that a successful type can enjoy an extremely long life. The Douglas DC-3 was an ageless design and in the modern era the Boeing 737 has been in production for over forty years, with each new model squeezing just a little more from the old core design. The Lockheed C130 Hercules has evolved through new engines, propellers and avionics amongst other things, but is still providing a critical niche in both military and civilian service. These types have been built upon for decades whereas the A380 and 787 sought to be revolutionary.

Revolutions may well serve the greater good, but when they go wrong someone can end up losing their head. The United Kingdom had the first commercial jet airliner to reach production in the form of the de Havilland Comet. With the loss of two aircraft and all on board, the Comet was grounded until the origin of the problem could be found. Simply put, the pressurisation cycles of the aircraft caused the corners of the square cabin windows to fail and catastrophically depressurise the aeroplane. Once the fault was discovered, the aircraft was fitted with the standard rounded windows we have today and the problem was seemingly overcome. However, in the midst of this both Boeing and Douglas took the advantage with the 707 and DC-8 respectively and Britain was relegated from world leader, destined never to regain the mantle.

To date, supersonic travel has been another costly frontier. Aerospatiale and the British Aircraft Corporation (BAC) formed a consortium to share the developmental burden of the Concorde. Undoubtedly a beautiful aeroplane, for one reason and another, it never assumed any dominance in the marketplace. It limped graciously through its majestic career until the crash of Air France Flight 4590, at Gonesse, France spelt the beginning of the end. By comparison, the Boeing 2707 Supersonic Transport (SST) became a costly venture and was ultimately retired before a prototype ever flew.

Both Boeing and Airbus have stepped away from their safety net in the development of their new machines. They could have opted for continuing to revamp and rejig members of their existing family, but the world cried out for more. Both companies responded to the call with the hope of landing a dominant blow upon the other, but both have suffered a series of painful jabs. Who will ultimately win the fight may come down to simply who can best deliver as opposed to a battle of philosophies. The sliding timetables were initially and fortunately offset by the global downturn. In a period where most airlines were shelving capacity, a line of new aeroplanes on the doorstep could have presented a whole new series of problems. This was luck, not planning and the wheel is now starting to turn.

For the sake of the industry, success by both Airbus and Boeing would be the best outcome. It would not only guard against a monopoly, but it would leave two long term players continuing to push the other to new boundaries with the likes of Embraer knocking on the door. Governments will always push the development of military aerospace and much of this technology will flow on to the civil ranks, but for conceptual change in the airline industry, the marketplace must speak. And their voice is best heard by more than one company.

Howard Hughes' Spruce Goose remains preserved and on display in Oregon, USA. It sought to achieve new heights but eventually barely lifted out of ground effect. Today Airbus and Boeing confront their own challenges as they endeavour to mould the next phase of airline travel in their projected image. It will be costly and there will be pain along the way, but for the future of airline travel, failure is not an option.

*****

27

Sleepless in Seattle

I was recently in Seattle, the home of Boeing, to ferry a brand new shiny 737-800 to Australia. It was my first visit to Washington State and the home of the sea-faring crab boats of the 'Deadliest Catch' fame and I must admit that I took an immediate liking to the city and its people. While the journey as a passenger took the best part of twenty four hours with a transit at Los Angeles, there was to be no rest for the wicked.

Arriving mid-afternoon, we were hosted that evening by the good folks at Boeing and received a wonderfully etched pair of drinking glasses to commemorate the hand-over and flight of the new 737. Yet as enjoyable as the evening was, it was the visit next day to the manufacturer's Everett facility and Boeing Field that really took my breath away. The size, the history and the atmosphere of the Boeing operation has to be seen to be believed.

The Everett facility is where the aeroplanes come together. The building which houses this 21st century example of Henry Ford's production line is the biggest building by volume in the world. Approaching it by vehicle, this gargantuan hangar just seems to keep on going with door after door featuring massive murals of the Boeing line. In turn, each of these doors is roughly the size of a football field! One feels very insignificant standing beside this monolith and yet the real magic takes place on the inside.

Within these walls a mass of components come together at one end of the building only to emerge as a completed aircraft at the other. In the case of the 737, Boeing are punching out the aircraft at a rate of one each day with plans to increase the number to 35 each month in 2012. While the rate of 787 production is nowhere near as rapid, it is equally fascinating to see the sleek lines of the composite airliner come together. If you like that new car smell, then the Boeing factory is somewhere that you should definitely add to your 'bucket list'.

Everything and everyone has a place. From the floor to the towering roof from which cranes hover, there are outlines and markings highlighting what belongs where. Each set of components and each bag of tools required to complete the day's task stands labelled and 'at the ready' on pristinely clean racks. Each item is meticulously accounted for, as a missing spanner or screw will bring the production line to a very expensive, screaming halt. For such a massive exercise in industry, the noise levels are amazingly low. There are no jack hammers or sprays of sparks, just highly trained professional teams assembling fine machinery to the most demanding tolerances. As a pilot, it evoked an even higher level of respect for the engineering that makes the miracle of flight possible.

Still in awe of what I had just witnessed, I was transported back towards downtown Seattle to visit the 'Museum of Flight'; another place for the 'bucket list'. Here there is a phenomenal collection of aircraft, civil and military, past and present, just as you'd expect in Boeing's hometown. There are warbirds galore, an original 'Air Force One' still with the President's trappings and a not-so-long retired Concorde. There are theatrettes, exhibitions and interactive displays to amaze and entertain, but there is something very, very special; the 'Red Barn'. The historic Red Barn, was the Boeing Company's original manufacturing plant built in 1909 and today forms one wing of the Museum of Flight. The artefacts within are phenomenal and include the first ever Air Mail bag and personal belongings of Elrey Jeppesen.

Yet for all of the treasured items, the Red Barn itself offers up a special kind of magic. Upstairs, the Chief Engineer's office remains as it was seventy years ago while downstairs the original tools of yesteryear and partially completed aircraft are attended to by mannequins dressed in the garb of a bygone era. For my money, a relatively empty room filled with benches stirs the imagination, for it was on these benches that ideas were translated into the reality of living flying machines. The walls now carry black and white images of draftsmen 'head down', slide rules and compasses in hand, frozen in time. Their faded images emit a real sense of pride and workmanship; something that is not lost on the Boeing workers of today. As I walked through the Everett facility and past the line of new 787s, that Boeing pride was still evident. The Dreamliner has not been without its issues and delays, but the manner of all those working there is very positive. There are banners marking development landmarks, signed by the staff that made it happen and constant reminders of where each developing airliner sits in the line of 787s waiting to fly the world.

From the workshop floor, to the Museum of Flight and the dinner with the people from Boeing, everything oozed professionalism. They were knowledgeable people at the top of their game, forging the future of commercial aviation. I could only imagine that Boeing would be a very positive, yet challenging place to be employed. This is a truly refreshing concept in an industry that can so often focus on the gloom and downside of its world.

For me, the trip to the home of Boeing was all too swift and yet I managed to gorge myself on much that it had to offer, as well as a significant number of delicious local crabs. It was a true privilege to take in both the history and future of commercial aviation surrounded by the people that make it possible. For me it was a trip that I'll always remember and just quietly, Meg Ryan can wait at the top of the Empire State Building because I found another special way to be Sleepless in Seattle.

*****

28

Heroes in our Midst

Through the course of my travels as both a pilot and writer, I have had the good fortune to encounter a vast array of interesting people; from Test pilots to Test cricketers, war heroes to war horses. Yet for all the remarkable tales I have listened to, it is so often the words between the sentences that capture the essence of the person. Those are the facts that so often fall between the cracks, or fade when the story is passed down to the next generation and beyond.

So often the manner in which a tale is told tells the greatest truths. There is emotion that may creep into the corner of a squinting eye, or a pause that admits that the perfect words can never truly be found. These men and women who have done such remarkable things often see themselves as commonplace and are caught off-guard by the inquisitive interest of a total stranger. Frequently, it is only decades later when life's long road offers perspective, that they can actually perceive that their undertakings were possibly more than ordinary. Up to that point they have been standing too close to the mirror.

I have spoken with war veterans who have had bullets whiz by within inches of their life and yet they never lost the focus of their task or their concern for their mates. Nurses that have smiled and cared for those who were beyond hope and elite athletes who vividly remember certain moments of solitude in the change room with far greater detail than the acts committed in front of the chanting masses. They are reticent and humble, deflecting any praise with humour, or attempting to pale their act by comparing it to the efforts of their peers.

I have never seen my role as levering these facts from the teller of the tale. My job is simply to listen. Sure, to have a knowledge of the subject matter, but above all, to listen. The enthralling events that grew into my first book 'Down to Earth' were gathered over endless cups of tea by a fireside, rather than probing interviews. The quieter that I sat, potentially the more revealing Squadron Leader Kenneth McGlashan became as he began to see his memories once again through the eyes of a young man. His friends came to life as a twinkle in his eye and the youthful excitement of that first aerial combat was relived once again. My task was to listen. Later I would collate, sort chronologically and rummage through historical records, but firstly I was there simply to listen.

Without exception these true heroes are great examples of humility. They are more likely to offer you scones and jam than a glimpse of their Distinguished Flying Cross or 'Baggy Green' cricket cap. I have found that if an individual has to tell you that they have the 'right stuff', generally they don't. Undoubtedly, deep within they carry a genuine pride, but they do not find the need to advertise or commercialise it. It is a quality that is so admirable, but also increasingly rare in an age where unfortunately fame seemingly outranks substance. Too often we now see the level of promotion of a deed in the media interpreted as the significance of the act. Unfortunately that is more closely related to 'spin doctors' and marketing savvy than it is to genuine accomplishment. For every 'hero in the headlines' there are hundreds going about their business, humming along and living their life without the need to be exalted or rewarded. These are the truest heroes.

Many heroes have died selflessly and their stories died with them on some foreign field. Others are happier hanging from a winch beneath a rescue helicopter, surrounded by crashing waves than they are facing the media. There are sporting heroes who find the greatest rewards are to be found through the smile of a sick child that their charity has helped, far away from the stadiums and studios.

Yes, true heroes live by action, not words. Generosity, not greed. Humility not hubris. Their memories and friendships are their truest treasure and should they sense the respect of their peers; well that is beyond their wildest dreams. These are special people, but they are hard to find. They may live in the wild as mothers or grandfathers, friends or teachers; you can never quite be sure. But should you encounter one in an unguarded moment, pause and listen; just listen. For they rarely speak of their deeds and should you be lucky enough to be there when they do, it is a very special day. Tread quietly out there my friends with your eyes and ears wide open. Look beyond the newspapers, magazines and televisions for it is only in those hidden corners of our world that you will find the heart of a true hero.

Yes, there are heroes in our midst.

*****

29

Love is in the Air

It is the final sector of a three day trip and I am climbing out of Adelaide and heading home. Behind me a line of low, dark clouds are rolling in from the Great Australian Bight as a cold front works its way towards ruining next weekend for the eastern states. But for the moment, all that lies ahead are blue skies and more friendly tailwinds.

As the Boeing's nose lowers at 35,000 feet and settles in for the run home we are made aware of some rather special news in the cabin. On board, a young gentleman is set to propose to his girlfriend when he steps off the aeroplane in Sydney. The cabin crew are excited and the news of the impending proposal brings a smile to my face that overrides the squint as I look into the morning sun. But wait, there's more...

The chap has brought on board sixty white roses and one red rose and they now sit silently in the chilled locker in the forward galley of the aircraft. His master plan is to have the disembarking passengers each hand his young lady a white rose before he finally emerges with the lone red rose, a ring and a very important question. Impressive! Well played young man.

Realising the effort that had gone into this proposal, we decided to play our part and help the process along, although making it any more special would always be a challenge. Before our base in Adelaide faded from radio range, we called them and advised them of the impending event at Sydney Airport and asked if they could call ahead and organise something special; perhaps even a camera or two.

The miles ticked along and one by one, Mildura, Wagga Wagga, Yass and Canberra slid by as the 'top of descent' grew near. Air Traffic Control gave us direct tracking to Sydney and requested our best speed on cruise and descent. Our schedule looked great with the touchdown time about fifteen minutes early, but would our efficient arrival throw out the best laid plans of our young suitor?

As the aerobridge docked and the door opened, our crew and wonderful passengers all played their part in the momentous day in this young couple's life. Although our shutdown checks and paperwork took precedence, it was apparent that the ball was in play. We could see the television camera crews through the expansive terminal windows and our passengers were moving up the aerobridge with blooms in hand.

By the time I emerged from the aerobridge there was one very excited young lady clutching armfuls of roses to a chorus of clapping strangers and cabin crew with iPhones armed and ready. On cue, the potential groom-to-be dropped to one knee and popped the question. She said "yes", the audience cheered and I'm pretty sure that I saw the young bloke breathe easily for the first time in a few hours.

I shook their hands and sincerely wished them all the best on their journey ahead. (Getting married was the smartest move I ever made.) As I left them to celebrate and made my way home I was hit once again by just how special my job can be. No two days ever seem quite the same and whether it is some spectacular glimpse of the sky from a new angle, or the chance to share a special moment in someone's life, aviation just seems to crack the door open to opportunity. It's then up to the individual to take it in and appreciate the wonder, or let the moment pass unrecognised. Personally, I think I will always opt to hold the moment in awe as long as I draw breath.

And while that weather front continued to creep across the inland and head east, the barometric pressure continued to drop. But for all the increasing relative humidity, frontal activity and turbulence, there are two people tonight that couldn't care less and will only ever remember that today, love was in the air.

*****

30

Look up and Live

What a week!

Six days straight of up and down from one side of the country to the other and back again. Finishing up with a nice little session in the flight simulator to validate that I am still proficient to sit up the front of the aeroplane; now I can look forward to a couple of days off. Days in which I can push the text books and manuals to one side and sit down and catch my breath. I love my job, but it's equally important to be able to switch off and wind down.

In the wake of a hectic day of simulated circling approaches and engine failures, I finally took time to pause. Lunch had been a cup of tea and a 'cookie' from the simulator centre's vending machine that had initially teetered reluctantly before falling to its death in the tray below. Now as I sat down to enjoy a peaceful meal, that elevated pace had subsided and I had time to relax.

I surveyed my fellow diners and a great many of them also looked relieved to have the day's work behind them. Coats removed and ties loosened, their posture was more closely related to slumping than sitting. A drink in one hand, one could almost hear the turbines in their skulls starting to spool down as they eased their grip on the day's affairs. Even so, one or two scanned their iPads and never raised their heads. Across the way another diner made his way to his seat, caught somewhere between his actual age and the trends of a boy-band. Needing a shave and a reminder that I didn't need to know what brand of underpants he wore, this individual thankfully pulled up his torn jeans a little before sitting down to thumb through the latest edition 'Vanity Fair'.

I had my favourite table by the window and chose that view as the backdrop to my wandering thoughts. For outside that window the clouds, sun and horizon were playing their afternoon game of hide and seek as nightfall approached. I never tire of the colours of dawn and dusk and the changing skyline of the Gods. Aviation has permitted me to witness this light show from many angles and altitudes on many occasions. Now as I dined, here was yet another as the bright orange rays dispersed into various hues of apricot and salmon amongst the stratus. While the towering cumulus gained an ominous edge as the impending darkness converted light to shadows.

A baby's squawk caught my attention and I revisited my fellow diners. The mother was desperately trying to keep her child quiet as if the baby's natural mechanisms were an affront to the sensibilities of others. I smiled at her and waved to the little girl, thinking of my own children and those wonderful dining experiences of rushed mouthfuls and stilted conversation. I smiled again, but this time at my own thoughts. Others still had their heads down over iPads as nature danced unnoticed outside the window. These same individuals would probably fight tooth and nail for the corner office, but if they looked up for a moment they would see that it was already here.

The waiter took my order and in no time I was enjoying my soup and sour-dough as the final rays of the day were beginning to be overwhelmed by the man-made lights of the city. What a sight it is, watching nature's time-lapse as day becomes night and back again. The meal comes and goes, but is almost overlooked as it is overshadowed by the world outside my window. A world that seemingly grows closer by the minute, ever-increasing in detail as the lights grow brighter.

Thump! Roaaarrrr..........

I am brought back to reality by the familiar sound of the engine's reversers coming to life and the strain on my seat belt under the forces of deceleration. The runway edge lights flash past as a blur and the flashing beacons of nearby aircraft punctuate the darkness. As quickly as it had announced itself, the roar subsides and the gentle rumble of the taxiway beneath is the only sound. As the cabin manager makes his announcement, the beacons of this jet now flash red against the scenery outside my window. I am advised that I am now free to switch on my phone, but pass on that option, content to gaze out the window for a few minutes more before the airport terminal's umbilical cord reaches out to the aeroplane and returns me to the real world.

And yet in this real world are the family and so many other things that I cherish, so the walk through the aerobridge is still upbeat. However, even as a passenger, or diner, the world aloft can still offer so much. Whether we are soaring through the stratosphere or land-locked on

157

the pavement, we can always look up from our iPads and cherish every moment.

*****

Jabiru Dawn at Kalbarri, Western Australia

Squadron Leader Kenneth Butterworth McGlashan AFC. (Image: McGlashan Collection)

31

ANZAC Dawn

It seems like it's always been the still dark hours. As those soldiers, the "ANZACS", prepared to land at Gallipoli and the armada positioned off Normandy, the peace of the night was juxtaposed against the human maelstrom that would unfold in only a matter of hours. Modern warfare has never known business hours and the bombings of Europe raged with equal vengeance through night and day. As a boy, the still dark hours came around for me every April 25th when it was ANZAC Day.

Each year that day was afforded special reverence in our home. Old photos of young faces were placed on the mantelpiece, with their smiles frozen in time. For these were the family and friends I never knew, but always felt that I did. My mother and father had both served in World War Two while my father saw action for a second time in Korea a few years later. Along the way so many of these fresh faces had perished; buried in some distant nation at best or their ultimate fate remaining unknown at worst.

My mother tended to the photographs, placing a small red poppy beside each of them and a relevant page of verse here or there. For my father's part, the faces stayed within his head and the photo albums in a bedroom cupboard. Yet despite their different forms of tribute, my parents never forgot those who had gone before and sacrificed their tomorrows. ANZAC Day was sacred in the Zupp household.

And in that dark household in those quiet hours before dawn I would be stirred from my bed by my parents; already dressed and ready for the day. As I dragged my young form into the land of the living my mother would fumble with the clasp holding her medals, while my father checked that his shoes were highly polished and his 'Returned from Active Service' badge was fastened in his lapel. His medals remained within his drawers for many years until I was on the verge of manhood when my mother finally had them mounted. His medals, like his service to his country, were treasured, but tucked away safely now that the job was done. Rather shy, he chose not to march on ANZAC Day, though he and my mother would always try to spot their mates on the television. For both my parents, the Dawn Service held the most significance and solemnity.

So each year we would climb into the car and sit on the cold, vinyl seats as we drove to the Cenotaph in the wee hours. The passing street lights were almost hypnotic to my drowsy eyes as we drove down the empty roads and finally parked. I would wake briskly as the car door swung open and the rush of April air bit my cheeks, before straightening up and following my parents passed barricades and attendants offering paper programmes. Groups of servicemen were in huddles, their breath forming small pockets of fog as they exchanged greetings and rubbed their hands together. Looking back, these men were younger than I am today and their war was far more recent than I ever realised. Yet to me they were old veterans in their grey suits and felt hats; men to be respected.

I would stand quietly with my parents with the silence only broken by the low hum of conversation, or the odd squawk of the bag-pipes as the kilted musician tuned his instrument. His legs must be so cold I used to think. Then the service would begin and the voices would cut through the silence without the need for microphones or amplification. I would listen intently and grasp what basic understanding I could of the importance of this service of remembrance.

As the service progressed through quotations, tributes and hymns, my father's jaw never flinched, nor did his sharp eyes ever seek the security of the ground ahead. However, my mother would have her quiet moments, drop her head silently and shed a tear, not knowing that I could see. My mother had lost her first fiancé in New Guinea only weeks before her wedding when his aircraft erupted in flames over the target. Her first Dawn Service had been only days after that loss in the dark, silent rain at the Sydney Cenotaph and she had missed very few Dawn Services since.

The 'Minute's Silence' would be so very, very silent that I dared not breathe until finally the bugle's Reveille would offer a reprieve and signal that the fallen had now been properly remembered. The men would once more move into groups, but now their conversation was less muffled; more open. They would head to the Returned Servicemen's Club for breakfast and the chance to reminisce before the ANZAC Day march. We would shuffle back to the car and have breakfast at home where Mum would share some significant recollections of the war and Dad would agree with her.

As we ate our breakfast, the photos always seemed to have another dimension after the Dawn Service and I viewed them in a slightly different light. I would look at the uniforms and the caps they wore more closely and stopped to realise just how young they really were in the overall scheme of life. In retrospect, it was all rather deep and philosophical for a boy of my age, but I suspect that's where the foundations for my strong sense of ANZAC Day was founded. And those faces have never left me.

In fact they are so much more than faces today. Their sacrifice stayed with me as I grew and I yearned to know more. Today, I have their photos in my home and their records of service sit on my desk. In fact, my own name hails from those of my father and one young face that was lost so many years ago. In recent years I have spoken to so many veterans and the families of those who served with my parents. I do my very utmost to ensure that their service and its significance is not lost in a world where celebrity seems to grab the headlines over substance at every turn. In the last year I was able to arrange for my children to meet with one of my father's squadron mates. A thorough gentleman, he is still as sharp as a tack and enthralled my children with tales of the grandfather they never knew. For me it was a truly special moment and a tangible link between my Dad and my beautiful family that further extended their pride in their Grandad.

Our veterans are special people, whether they served long ago, or if they are currently sweating it out in Uruzgan Province in Afghanistan. Whether they failed to return, or survived to tell the tale. Whether they lie in a marked grave or perished without trace in some dark jungle. They all made a sacrifice for the freedoms we possess today and so often take for granted.

After meeting my father's air force comrade that day, we also visited the Australian War Memorial and walked along the rows of names enshrined on its walls. My oldest daughter began to grasp the enormity of what these names represented, while my young son raced along the pathway. As I went to bark at him to slow down in such a sacred aisle, I paused just for a moment. His grandfather and so many had served so that he could be free to run in the shadow of these sacred names. Even so, without my raised voice he came to an abrupt halt and stared at the plaque ahead of him. The plaque bore the names of those killed in service with 77 Squadron in the skies over Korea.

That was my father's squadron.

Lest We Forget.

*****

32

Best Seat in the House

The day's only a few hours old and the sun sits low out to the left hand side. The morning air is still as we head south along the Australian seaboard, bound for Sydney at 37,000 feet. It's one of those days when you can see forever and every detail of the earth below is crystal clear. The Queensland township of Emerald sits off the nose, moving ever closer at a deceptively high rate while Bundaberg approaches to the east. My mind recalls the morning two years ago when I set course from Bundy for Emerald on the first leg of my solo flight around the country.

On that occasion I sat much closer to the earth and the wonderful little aeroplane clipped along at two miles each minute, rather than hurtling along at 450 knots as I now find myself. As I look down on the cultivated chessboard that is rural Australia, I can almost see the little white wings of the Jabiru far below taking its first steps on that 13,000km journey. Back then, ahead lay two astounding weeks of sights, sounds and scenery at an altitude where you often felt that you could reach out and touch the wonders you were witnessing.

By comparison, Flight Level 370 is far more removed. It is the same beautiful land beneath my wings; however the perspective is vastly different. From this height I can see the cavernous mines gouged out of the earth, while they may well have slipped by unnoticed, obscured by rising ranges either side of the Jabiru. And even those ranges look different from on high. They are mere ripples in the landscape, whose ribbon-like rock faces are illuminated by the morning sun. To the Jabiru these were towering walls that exuded details of their history, forged up from the young planet and then worn down by the weather of time. Jagged edges, precipitous drops, smooth faces and a spectrum of colours that could fill the windscreen, all appear as an inconspicuous stripe from way up here.

As my finger tracked along the topographical map and my other hand kept the Jabiru steady, I would scan left and right for features. Lakes, dams, power lines, roads and airstrips would all serve to guide my way as two miles of the outback blanket passed beneath every minute. From the upper atmosphere the real world looks like a chart laid out below as my eyes trace along the roads and other notable features. Everything is there to see as the flight management computer and autoflight system guide the Boeing homeward at Mach 0.78. Some townships represent little more than a white square on the predominantly green and brown quilt of the countryside, while power lines are invisible. The roads and tracks criss-cross like a system of arteries and capillaries supplying the land with its life-blood. At fifteen hundred feet you could see the dust kicked up from the wheels of a motorcycle.

Even my own aeroplane's shadow is vastly different. From 37,000 feet it is an oddly lit patch of light racing across the paddocks where the Boeing has disturbed the sun's spectrum. To the backdrop of a cloud, it is a flash of the aircraft's form, often surrounded by its own halo of rainbow colours. Low down, the Jabiru's shadow was a constant companion; never far away. A crisp outline of the high-winged tourer was always there with me, skipping over fences and tree-lines at break-neck speeds and drawing ever closer on the approach to land until the two forms again reunited and merged when the wheels finally touched the runway.

As I change frequencies and switch off the centre tank fuel pumps, I long for that freedom of the solo flight again and yet, I appreciate the view from the flight deck as well. For regardless of altitude, the earth below is a majestic place, only the perspective changes. Down low you can see every stitch in the landscape, while at 37,000 feet you are free to take in the overwhelming beauty of the entire tapestry. And even when you think that you have seen it all, the sunlight, the weather or the seasons change and a whole new range of colours and contours are highlighted.

I never tire of the view from my office and the size of it has no bearing on my enjoyment. Whether seated behind a spinning propeller or pushed along by 52,000lb of relatively quiet thrust, it doesn't matter a bit. Whether there is someone there to bring me a coffee, or I'm chewing on a muesli bar from my backpack, I couldn't care less. It is not the cabin's furnishings that we come to see, but the glory that sits outside the window and reminds us of why we fly. High or low, fast or slow, the view from the cockpit is to be cherished as it is undoubtedly the best seat in the house.

*****

33

Up Close and Personal.

As It was not just another day at the flight school – the film cameras were testament to that. In the pre-dawn darkness, the normally mundane act of pushing open hangar doors was met with the dramatic silhouette of an aircraft lit by stage lights, radiating their beams from behind. The artificial sunrise illuminated the hangar within and I knew that the clanging of sliding hangar doors was destined to be dubbed over with romantic orchestral chords once the film was produced.

The footage was to promote the wonders of Australia and its idyllic setting for pilot training. The first sortie would fly over the famous harbour in Sydney, highlighted by the coat hanger-like bridge and the iconic opera house. The second formation flight would head west over a rural pastures, rugged ranges and expansive dams. But first the aircraft needed to be readied.

Beyond the hangar, torchlight beams cut through the darkness as pilots unlashed aeroplanes from their land-locked moorings and began preparing them for the flights ahead. Dawn was just a dim glow in the east, but already the crews had attended a full briefing and submitted flight plans. The intent was to take to the skies early, in the calm air and the best light.

Of the five pilots, three had military training and two of those had flown jet fighters. One had flown in combat. That pilot was my father and today he would fly in the seat beside me to complete my training in formation flying. The experience that surrounded me was a little intimidating, but that feeling would soon be lost to the demands of flying in close proximity to another aircraft.

As the propellers began to crank, the mild eruption of the engines broke the silence of the airport. Blinking red beacons and white taxi-lights cut through the crisp dark air as the two-seater trainers taxied out with the camera ship to the rear. The sun had broken the horizon by the time the engines had warmed and the checks were completed and the aircraft lined up on the runway.

I sat to the rear and to the left of the leader, lining up the visual cues on his aircraft and mine that I had defined previously using parked aircraft. On the leader's call we throttled up and then released the brakes. Every bump in the runway seemed to be magnified as the leader bounced and accelerated. And then his nose wheel lifted off and mine followed suit, easing into the air and endeavouring to hold 'station' steadily and with minimal movement of the throttle.

The air was like glass as we wheeled to the north and over the suburbs before tracking east towards the coast. All the while I concentrated with every ounce of my mental might, while my father sat relaxed and content beside me. He reminded me that it was a long day ahead and encouraged me to loosen the formation until we approached the harbour, when the cameras would be rolling. I backed off and edged my aircraft away from the leader just a little. That slightly greater spacing allowed me to take in the scenery below and the beautiful rising sun.

The golden rays bounced of the fuselage of the leader as the camera ship made an appearance here and there, up-sun and seeking out the best angle and light. I marvelled at seeing another aircraft in its realm at such close quarters. Without any relative movement, it seemed to just sit there, truly defying gravity and with no apparent urgency to have rushing airflow over its wings to create lift. Of course, it was still carving its path through that air, but as I sat nearby it seemed so still, so peaceful.

My father too seemed at peace. I wondered how many times he had sat off the wing of another – probably too many times to count, including days when the flak and ground fire had filled the air. Like the aircraft itself, he too was at home when he was aloft. There were no phone calls or street-level dramas, just the purity of flight. I looked at the creases around across his leathery face and wondered if I would ever be so at home in the skies. Only time would tell.

The serenity was interrupted by air traffic control advising us that our flight over the harbour would be delayed and that we could hold east of the coast and clear of his airspace. On such a brilliant morning, such news isn't particularly disappointing. As we dawdled about the sky, the leader broke away before starting an increasing arc back towards us in a manoeuvre that my father interpreted as the beginning of a dog-fight. On his call of "Taking Over!" the little trainer rolled towards his foe and the two ex-military men engaged each other in mock combat. With the weight of two on board our aircraft, we had a decided disadvantage, but somehow we rolled and twisted inside the

170

other aircraft and won the 'battle'.

The fight was over in the blink of an eye and for a moment my father had lit up as if he were a boy. My world was still spinning at the speed at which he had moved from calm to combat and back to calm. He handed over control to me once more and he peered out the window with a distinct smile threatening the corner of his mouth.

With the way clear we approached the harbour and now my father urged me to "tuck in tighter" and reassured me that "you won't hit him". Initially, I sat in the 'line astern' position behind the other trainer holding his rudder steady above and ahead as we entered the harbour, moving back out to the side as the opera house loomed ahead. The camera ship above and the amazing scenery beneath did not enter my thoughts or vision. My focus was purely on the leader and my aircraft relative to him. The camera ship made teasing comments about how spectacular the setting was, but I dared not drift my eyes away from the task at hand. The enjoyment level was high, but so was the fatigue as I was still learning this craft and trying to fly as smoothly as possible. The minutes raced by and with the camera ship and air traffic control satisfied, we set course for our home base.

We held the formation as we approached the airfield and lowered our flaps in synchronisation. Ready for the landing my eyes scanned between the leader and the side of the runway on which I was to land. The scan continued all the way until my wheels touched the ground just as leader's did, before we slowed and I slipped in behind him for the taxi back to the flight school, raising our flaps in time with one another.

Shutting down our engines, I felt both dehydrated and weary. I don't think had ever concentrated so solidly in an aeroplane and wished for the time that formation flying would become just a little easier. For the moment, there was only time to replenish and re-brief the second sortie before we would be underway once again.

The second take-off seemed easier, aided by the heavier, faster aircraft we were flying. Retracting the wheels on the leader's command must have looked impressive as it drew a complement from the control tower as we climbed away past his vantage point. The green fields slid by and the mountain range lay ahead. In contrast to the aqua harbour and the city skyline, the backdrop was now one of dark green foliage and the reservoir's deep blue waters.

The dam wall stood tall with lines of water running down its face as we set course along pristine valleys and flew past the jutting rock formation of 'The Three Sisters'. The camera ship called for a turn here or a turn there to maximise its perspective, but still I just stayed focussed on the leader and his wing. With his wheels tucked up the aircraft looked so speedy and sleek and the scenery was just a blurred background most of the time. However, the detail on the aircraft itself was close at hand – the leader's headset, the small aerials and the occasional minimal movement of the control surfaces were all crystal clear. Up close and personal and loving it.

When the director called in that enough footage had been gained, we turned for home and once again landed in formation with the camera rolling and my pulse racing. By the time we had shutdown I was wet with sweat and ready for rest, while my father was at ease in spite of the constant tuition I had drawn from him. He had been in his environment and seemed disappointed to be reunited with the earth.

Back in the briefing room we ran through the details of both flights. What were the strengths and would could have been flown better? Were there any lessons to be learned apart from those that my father had in store for me? As I looked around at the experience in my midst I felt privileged to have be trained in the skill by their like. Understated and extremely competent, I learned a good deal more than the manipulative aspects of formation flying that day – these men were aviators. And that night I slept like never before.

These pilots would regroup again months later, but things would be very different. There would be no briefing for me and I would watch from the ground as I heard their imminent arrival overhead. Their first pass was immaculate – a tight vee-formation that had the gathered crowd looking skyward, their excitement shared in silent awe.

The trio tracked around the horizon and every eye was locked upon them as they lined up for their final pass. The three aircraft grew nearer and nearer and then, just as they arrived, one pulled vertically into the sky and peeled away from the formation in a manoeuvre known as the 'Missing Man'.

Not a word was spoken and tears ran down many cheeks, for this was a farewell. My father had passed and this was their final salute to the old fighter pilot. He was now at home in the heavens.

*****

34

The Eagle has Landed

It's not as if it was yesterday, but the memory is still etched firmly in my mind. I am five years old, cross-legged on the living room floor in front of our black and white television, mounted in its polished cabinet. A scratchy signal was being beamed to the earth from the moon, where on the Sea of Tranquility, a 38 year old from Ohio was about to create world history.

The actions of Neil Armstrong and his Apollo 11 crew of Buzz Aldrin and Mike Collins on that day have been revisited so many times from so many angles. His famous lines, "The Eagle has landed" and "One small step..." have entered the vocabulary of millions and been pirated more times than could ever be tracked. But there was so much more to Armstrong than those few very important steps.

He flew nearly eighty combat missions during the Korean War, ejecting in one instance after his aircraft was hit by ground fire and a very stationary pole! He earned a Masters degree in Aeronautical Engineering and always regarded his engineering background as one of his primary achievements, teaching the subject at University in later life.

He was a test pilot at Edwards Air Base in the days of the "Right Stuff". He was heavily involved in the X-15 project and flew that aircraft beyond 200,000 feet and five times the speed of sound. He became an astronaut on the Gemini program, undertaking a complex rendezvous and docking manoeuvre in space on Gemini 8. Armstrong was the back-up Commander for Gemini 11, but when not needed, served as the Capsule Communicator or CAPCOM, for the mission. He ejected at low altitude from the cumbersome Lunar Landing Training Vehicle, or "Flying Bedstead". He was a husband and as a father, lost a child at a young age. This all occurred before he ever set foot on the Moon.

Apollo 11 and the Moon landing are still captivating today for so many reasons. It was part of a 'space race' that saw the West pitted against the East. Its conception evoked historic words from John F. Kennedy, even though he would not live to witness his dream. It would drive a nation in a unified cause while the war in Vietnam sought to tear it apart.

Apollo 11 came to represent the incredible technological advances of the twentieth century. Even though man had only taken to the air in powered flight six decades earlier, he was now kicking up moon-dust and planting flags. It seemed that anything was possible with the right people, resources and will-power. This sentiment drew 500 million to watch their television sets in 1969 and has inspired billions ever since.

And at the centre of this world-embracing mission were three men and one of those would be the first to step upon the surface. In doing so, Armstrong both catapulted himself into history and strapped the burden of fame to his back. The years would show that he could handle both with the intelligence and grace that had earmarked him as something special at an early age. He did not ask for the unending attention and in fact avoided it on many occasions, for he, better than anyone realised that he was but one man.

Before he could descend down that ladder and say those immortal words, thousands of others had played their role for his moment in the spotlight. Friends had died, including Grissom, White and Chaffee who had burnt to death in their capsule on the launch pad during a test. So many people, so many hours, so many taxpayer dollars to make the impossible happen and then it all came down to three men.....and in the end, just one.

When he neared the lunar surface and saw boulders strewn across his landing site, he took the module out of full automatic control and guided it to safety. Low on fuel with Aldrin calling out descent data he brought the Eagle down to land with only seconds of fuel remaining. In those final moments, Apollo 11 came down to nerves of steel and the Grace of God. The world watched on and held their breath, but history was to show that it was in good hands.

Armstrong left the module and as the first human foot was placed on the surface of the Moon, he uttered that immortal phrase, "That's one small step for man. One giant leap for mankind." And while some have argued whether there was an "a" somewhere in that sentence, the spirit of the statement places such debates on the top of the list of useless trivia. Man had achieved what had seemed impossible only decades before.

And so Armstrong, for better or worse, carried the banner for what many considered to be man's greatest achievement. He has had buildings, awards, scholarships and all host of things named in his honour. He has had his autographed forged and sold by so many profiteers that he ultimately ceased signing his name. The Moon landing was the world's pride and joy, but beneath its enormity lay one man's life.

The day that we lost Neil Armstrong I had been speaking about him, totally unaware of his passing. For me, I think the moment that I learned of his death will remain one of those pivotal moments in my life when I will always remember where I was. Fittingly I was sitting on the flight deck of a Boeing 737 with the towering snow-capped mountains of Queenstown, New Zealand all around me. I felt a twinge of sentiment at the news and I am not one that is generally prone to such reactions. And why? I didn't know Neil Armstrong.

But he was there as I sat cross-legged as a five year old in front of my television and he had been there ever since. Apollo 11 and Armstrong, Aldrin and Collins showed me that anything was possible and that the dream of flight knows no bounds. And as I have looked to the heavens, his sky was my sky, his stars were my stars, but when I looked to the moon, it was always his.

The Eagle has landed.

God Speed, Commander.

*****

35

Joie de Vivre

Sometimes you can just be downright lucky. Occasionally a magical blend of the history, pleasure and pure joy of flight can combine to create one of those memorable moments aloft. For me, such an event took place only yesterday.

As I departed my home airfield, my hopes for the day ahead weren't terribly high despite the clear skies above. As I lifted my little aeroplane into buffeting 40 knot winds, I considered the effect that the blustery breeze would have upon the treasured vintage aircraft that I was scheduled to fly. Despite its proud bearing, the 1943 Stearman is still a tailwheel biplane and these conditions would surely make every moment a challenge. And yet, as I commenced descent towards my coastal destination the rocking and rolling of the turbulence dissipated and I went from being thrown in the harness to smoothly slipping down towards the circuit pattern.

The airfield sat in a basin, shadowed from the confronting westerly winds. Bordered on one side by rolling green pastures it was mirrored by the coastline on the other. As I touched down, there was no doubt that this was one of those perfect days to commit aviation and as I turned off the taxiway and came to a halt, the scarlet Stearman stood before me. Tall and proud, the beautiful biplane sported finely crafted 'nose art' of a scantily clad lass and the words "Lilly Warra" painted nearby as a tribute to the Illawarra district that the aeroplane now called home. But beauty was far more than skin deep for this veteran of a war from long ago.

Just as her paint scheme was striking, so too was her heritage. For this old girl had once been a faithful trainer to the famed 'Red Tails'; the Tuskegee Airmen. Many miles had passed beneath her wings in the past seven decades and I only wished those wings could speak. Even so, as I slipped into the cockpit and strapped into the harness, I felt a sense of awe as if I had stepped through the fragile fabric of time. With my canvas helmet strapped beneath my chin and my goggles pulled firmly down over my eyes, I scanned the comfortable cocoon around me. The strong metal frame was not hidden by any lining, but encased me in a secure maze of piping and cables, while a bare minimum of dials and levers were there to guide her through the sky.

Ahead lay the shining cylinders of the radial engine, void of a cowling and open to the cooling breeze. The hand-crafted wooden propeller responded to the call of the starter and kicked over as the engine caught the shower of sparks and burst into life. A puff of smoke and its accompanying smells wafted back past the cockpit as the engine gained increasing momentum as one by one the cylinders rose to the occasion in a throbbing harmony.

If the introduction was an honour then the moment of flight was magical. The throttle was only open for a matter of seconds and the tail rose to offer a view of the runway ahead. As I eased the stick back towards me with a touch of rudder to assist, my magic carpet eased into the air and I turned towards the coast. All of my senses were alive as the breeze passed through the bracing wires and the slipstream glanced my cheeks with just a faint scent of combustion. I felt safely at one with this stable steed, whose harmonies made the flying machine seem more like a living creature than a mere aeroplane.

Outside the cockpit the world slid by, illuminated by the brilliant sunshine of early spring that drew out the richness of every single colour. The deep blue-green of the water as it licked the yellow sand and the stark whiteness of the lighthouse against the backdrop of the jade headland. People were out and about with picnic baskets and blankets and all of them seemed to pause and cast their eyes upward to sight the crimson craft crossing their sky. The world was a perfect place at that moment. With a touch of rudder followed by a squeeze of the stick, the horizon wheeled around in front of me and a trio of pelicans soared past with an equal amount of grace.

A series of loops and 'lazy eights' made the world dance graciously from a variety of viewpoints. The aerobatics of a Stearman are decidedly 'gentlemanly' for a lady of the skies. No heaving or hauling, just a sweeping pattern that gently carries those on board through all three dimensions of flight. For over an hour I experienced the best that man, machine and the Maker could offer and I breathed it all in as deeply as I could. These were moments to cherish.

These moments eventually had to end and as the painted numbers on the runway's threshold loomed ahead I felt both excitement and sadness; I wanted this flight to last forever. But the real world and fuel tanks don't allow such a thing, so I settled for smoothly closing the throttle and returning "Lilly" back to the earth. I cycled the rudder pedals to keep straight and it seemed that like me, the Stearman wasn't done yet. Finally, the tail settled, the view ahead disappeared and we taxied in and shut the engine down.

As the propeller swung to a halt with the magnetos switches off, I paused for a moment. I just sat there. I reflected upon the sheer sense of pleasure, while still feeling as relaxed as I could ever imagine. Again I breathed the moment in and it tasted sweet. I thought how privileged I was that in a world of pressing schedules and commitments I could step back to 1943; a very different time. And then, from the best seat in the house I was able to dawdle about the sky with no particular place to go and no particular time to be there.

These are moments to cherish. This is the purest essence of flight. The sheer enjoyment of life, or should I say, "Joie de vivre".

*****

Joie De Vivre! The scarlet Stearman over the waves. (Image: Australian Aviation)

Flight Testing the Cozy Mark IV. (Image: Australian Aviation)

36

Leap of Faith

Bald Hill at Stanwell Park in Australia is much less than inconspicuous. From a car driving past, if you blink, you'll miss it. Even when you stand upon its crest with the ocean's waves crashing far below, it is a small patch of mown grass that very quickly turns to rough scrub and falls away dramatically. Between the strong winds, limited space and the precipitous drop, only the very bravest would dare to gather the family for a picnic on Bald Hill. And yet it is a very special place.

For over a century ago Lawrence Hargrave used this small hill as the launching pad for his pioneering work in the world of aerodynamics. For many Australians, Hargrave was most widely known as the man whose image was to be found on the twenty dollar note, while Sir Charles Kingsford Smith adorned the flip side. With a change in the design of the currency, his image and name has faded, but in the world of aviation he remains a true pioneer in the quest for manned flight.

On November 12th 1894 Hargrave secured himself to a chain of his 'box kites' and rose to a height of five metres above the beaches below Bald Hill. A major step in the search for heavier-than-air flight, Hargrave had made significant advances in the study of curved aerofoils, box-kites and rotary engine development. A firm believer in the sharing of scientific knowledge, he never sought to patent any of his discoveries or designs. Consequently, his findings were incorporated in designs all around the world and the history of early manned flight is littered with its pioneers paying credit to Lawrence Hargrave.

Yet for many, Hargrave's name will draw a blank response, but as I stand on Bald Hill, his legacy is all around me. In a traditional sense there is a monument to the man, albeit missing its bronze plaque which has mysteriously disappeared. However, his legacy survives in a far more tangible form as Bald Hill is now home to the modern 'bird men'; the hang-gliders. One by one they assemble their basic rigs and leave the grassy knoll for the freedom of the skies. At times the sky is filled with their triangular forms sailing upon the breeze; from a virtual hover to surfing downwind at speed.

As I observe their airborne dance it takes very little effort to imagine Hargrave's spectre standing beside me, undoubtedly filled with joy. His scientific mind would have seen the parallels of the aerodynamic form to his early studies and he would have stood in awe of their control and freedom. A sense of the breeze and a shift of weight and the hang gliders soar about the ridge line in the purest form of flight. Airliners climb out overhead bound for the southern states and their backdrop only further highlights the advances that aviation has made. And I think I can see Hargrave's jaw dropping just a touch as he looks to the heavens.

With their landing fields on the beaches far below, I take the land-borne route via the steep, winding road and await the gliders arrival with my young son. He squints as he scans the bright sky for the colourfully adorned triangles and tracks them with an outstretched, pointing hand. Such a pure form of silent flight, he leans his ear towards the wind as the words of those above waft down to the earth. We are both entranced by these dancing descendants of Hargrave's humble box-kites as one after the other they position themselves above the beach. Their touch-down resembles a bird's landing as their graceful flight transitions by means of a pair of legs running along the surface until they slow down and once again bear the weight of gravity's burden.

I am in awe of this form of flight and feel the very history seeping up through the grains of sand beneath my feet; the same sands that Lawrence Hargrave once hovered above. I cast my gaze back up to Bald Hill and sight his monument jutting up from the rounded ridge and in my mind's eye I can see Hargrave there with his kites sailing on the wind. I am brought back to reality serenely as another glider leaves the certainty of the ground and moves into the mystical beauty of the air. Just as Hargrave once had, another seeks to soar above Stanwell Park and make the skies their own through a wonderful leap of faith.

*****

37

Mustangs and Memories

Once in a while you get the opportunity to tear up the sky in something a little out of the ordinary. And ain't it great!

As the four flat blades slowly turned, reality was now sinking in. I was strapped in, low and tight, in the rear of a World War Two vintage fighter; the 'Mustang'. As the vapour searched for spark, the Merlin engine pushed the blades to an ever-increasing speed. Fuel, air and ignition then found common ground and the whirring blades were replaced by the throaty roar of 12 cylinders leaping in to life. The exhaust stacks punched out a burst of smoke that caught a ride in the slipstream and wove its way into the still-open cockpit. Ahead of display pilot Guy Bourke's helmet, the propeller now formed a huge disc as the moving parts settled into a harmony and after start checks were completed.

It was thirty years since I'd last sat low and tight in a Mustang's cockpit. At eight years of age there were very few other ways to sit. My father had hoisted me into the cockpit of the retired fighter as it sat in the darkened confines of Syd Marshall's Air Museum at Bankstown Airport. Ever since his RAAF days, the Mustang had been my father's favourite. More than the Meteor jets he had flown in Korea, or the Super Connies in which he'd criss-crossed the globe; it was always the Mustang. Leaning in, he explained the numerous dials and switches with military thoroughness. The systems and limitations poured forth from his razor sharp memory that would still forget to pick up milk on the way home. I grasped what I could, but found my imagination drifting elsewhere. My head revolving as it moved its gaze from the enormous cowling ahead back to 'check my six'….just in case.

Now an adult, I once again found myself swivelling at the neck. It was an air-show day at a regional aviation museum and the atmosphere was charged. Taking in the sights and sounds of this fantastic opportunity, I spotted my wife in the crowd. In conspiracy with a chap I'd known for years, Guy Bourke, she had secretly arranged the wedding anniversary gift of a lifetime. I had never seen my wife so keen for me to go to an air-show and her reasoning was now very apparent. The flight was to be made up of two sections. The first involved an air-to-air photo shoot in company with another fighter, the Australian Boomerang, and a trainer of yesteryear, the North American Harvard. At the conclusion of this sortie, 'Bourkey' and I would break off and take the Mustang to the west on its own. This had been briefed thoroughly pre-flight and the Harvard now led the three ship formation out to the end of Runway 36.

Checks complete, we sat beneath the closed canopy awaiting our turn for take-off. The aft seat had a Spartan instrument panel of an altimeter and airspeed indicator to the right. To the left, at about the same height, was the throttle quadrant. Ahead, the control column and rudder pedals complete the picture. As the pristine Boomerang cleared the perimeter fence, Guy announced our departure and smoothly increased the abundant power of the V12 engine. I have been fortunate to fly a number of aircraft over the years, but the sounds, sensations and sinking into the seat of a Mustang take-off takes some beating. As rudder authority increased with airflow, the tail was raised to introduce a new world of enhanced visibility. The ground rush in the peripheral vision began to change in focus as the ground fell away and the gear was selected up. All clear for the turn, Bourkey rolled this fierce piece of North American design to the left in pursuit of the formation. Closing on the two specs at an impressive rate, one couldn't help but imagine how many times this scene had been acted out in skies around the world in a very different time. With the Harvard serving as the camera ship, we slotted in to the right of the Boomerang. Sitting tight on the little Aussie fighter, it was easy to see every rivet on its immaculate surface. After weaving across the skies in formation for a period, it was time to break right and head west on our own.

The land surrounding this airfield is custom built for committing aviation. Golden fields of crops, uninterrupted by the rising terrain that can so often pose a problem. Should all go quiet 'up front', potential landing fields are numerous, offering a special type of peace to the single-engine pilot. It is little wonder that this site was chosen as an Elementary Flight Training School throughout the war years and was home to a flock of Tiger Moth biplanes. Set to this backdrop Guy climbed the Mustang to a safe height and set about demonstrating some rolls and loops. Even tucked into the back seat, the brilliant visibility afforded by the bubble canopy allows tremendous orientation throughout the manoeuvres. As sky passed earth and back to sky, a sense of balance and power pervaded the aircraft. It was in its realm and roared across the heavens with the freedom of its namesake. I gratefully accepted control on Guy's call of, "Handing Over" and proceeded to experience that freedom first hand. I exercised the controls and the Mustang responded crisply to the inputs. Seemingly unencumbered by adverse yaw to any degree, the rudder is used as a tuning fork rather than a backhoe. Scanning the horizon and the skies, the aircraft holds the attitude as if set in stone and I take in the view and the ambience.

All too soon, the minutes have ticked over and Terra Firma calls. We set the airfield in the windscreen and call inbound for an 'initial and pitch' entry, Runway 36. Circuit-side and parallel, we zoom along the bitumen before pulling up and left to enter the circuit. Power steady, the energy is managed and the drag deployed to position the aircraft on left base. Final calls, final checks and the Mustang sets its sights on the touchdown point under Guy's hand. Over the fence, powering back and the wide track of the main gear reunites Man and Mustang with Mother Earth. As the speed washes off, the tail slowly lowers and the back of Guy's helmet again dominates my field of view.

The exhilaration as we taxied in was hard to harness. Mindful of wingtip clearance, we navigated through a tarmac littered with a gallery of aircraft that I could only admire. In position and checks complete, power is withdrawn from this great machine and the huge disc dissipates to again form four distinct blades. Becalmed, with 'switches off', the adventure is over. A childhood dream had been realised and it had lived up to all expectations. As I took in the moment, I was that eight year-old once again, strapped in low and tight and looking back to 'check my six' one more time......just in case.

38

A Long Way to Hollywood

As I sit in yet another hotel room in yet another town, the setting is almost too familiar. I pause for a moment to contemplate this nomadic lifestyle choice and cast my mind to the many different sunrises and cities that aviation has afforded me over the years. For the by-product of many hours aloft are numerous nights away from home and with that comes so many different experiences; from the shearing sheds at Murchison Station in Western Australia to the Champs-Elysees in Paris.

However, it has not always been a case of well-appointed hotel rooms on the 26th floor. Starting out in aviation was far from such luxury, but in some ways it was richer in character. As a young pilot I lived in a caravan in the outback Kimberley region, so any hotel room was a step up in quality. It was a time in my career and my life when my worldly possessions fitted snugly into the boot of a Toyota Corolla and I could move onto the next town, or job, at a moment's notice if needed. Yet, rather than my lodgings, it was those nights away from home that often threw up the memorable moments in a variety of ways. Even the climate could play a role in the making of memories.

One clear evening, fatigued and 'out of hours' I parked my twin-engined Cessna at Hall's Creek, just south of my home base at Kununurra. With nothing but a bag of charts, I walked a couple of miles to the 'chopper farm' where our company's mustering pilots would camp for the night. Inside laid a bed, but no bedding, as the chopper pilots carried their own blankets, or 'swag'. That night I lay in my uniform and froze through fitful patches of sleep waiting for the sun to return.

By contrast, I sweltered on a camp stretcher in New Guinea in a hut near the Fly River. As the beads of sweat soaked through, I could hear the sloshing of the crocodiles in the reeds only a stone's throw from my door. Earlier that night I had consumed a meal of shrimp and eel caught from within those reeds and boiled up with a generous bowl of rice. I was so hungry that day and despite much fine dining in the years since, that meal still remains one of the best that I've ever eaten.

I've slept under the wing from time to time and it isn't quite as romantic as it sounds. Prone on the cold ground with the dew dripping down is not the setting for relaxed slumber. Not to mention that the same dew drops offer up a drummers beat in the case of a fabric biplane as each drop reverberates on hitting the bottom wing, having fallen from the top. And yet there is something magical about the stars when they're viewed from such humble accommodation. Airfields are isolated places and with nothing but an aeroplane and the occasional wildlife bounding by, the solitude offers time for real reflection. It even offers a slight insight into the life of the cowboys and drovers from so many years ago; camping by the track with just a saddle and their swag. However, for me, civilisation was a mere "Clear Prop!"

and an hour's flight time away.

The cockpit was only marginally more comfortable than sleeping beneath the wing. One night on Manus Island, with nowhere to sleep and a growing suspicion of the intentions of the locals who had refuelled my twin-engined Islander, I opted to sleep in the pilot's seat. If the cabin had not been filled with ferry tanks full of fuel, there would have been a great deal of room to lie down; but there wasn't. Even so, the left hand seat provided a sheltered, if cramped, place to rest and I've always been able to find sleep wherever I may be. In contrast, having flown the Islander to Micronesia the next day I sat by the most pure azure waters I have ever seen. As they sloshed up on the beach, my hut was only metres away and the memory of that tropical paradise and treasures of its jungles and lagoons still beckons me back thirty years later.

With a career in the airlines came four walls, air-conditioning and room service. At first it was novel, but soon it became all too familiar. At the same time, I appreciated where these 'five star cells' were located and set my mind to using the time fruitfully. I would use some of the downtime to complete university assignments and meet writing deadlines However, beyond the foyer was a world of museums, shows, galleries and cuisines that I never could have imagined growing up in a small fibro home in western Sydney. The hotel room where I slept became more of a transit lounge as I sought to consume all the culture that surrounded me.

The people and places of the world expanded my horizons in a way I had never experienced. As a bush pilot, I had seen so much of Australia and its culture at its grass roots and now the airlines showed me the world. This was one of the 'positives' to come out of an airline collapse that otherwise saw my career stall and fall. My very first trip as an international pilot was to Paris when a few weeks before I had been sitting in the unemployment agency. In one day I criss-crossed Paris until my legs could take me no further. The River Seine, the Eiffel Tower, the Moulin Rouge, the site of the Bastille, the Arc de Triomphe and on and on and on.......

Elsewhere in the world, London was my favourite city and again it was the history that enthralled me. From castles to Shakespeare's Globe Theatre, old taverns and air shows. There just never seemed to be enough time to take it all in. San Francisco was my pick of the US west coast destinations and reminded me so much of Sydney, except for the presence of Alcatraz Prison sitting on its island in the Bay. By contrast, Los Angeles had seemingly little to offer, although the desk at which I would sit to write often stared straight at the famous Hollywood sign. In L.A. I would opt to hire a car and drive away from down-town at every opportunity. The best days were spent on the road driving through Orange County or the compulsory visits to Chino Airport and a coffee at Flo's to the sound of warbirds roaring overhead.

For this nomad it has indeed been a fortunate life and yet as I get older, I long for home more and more. For once the love and stability of a family life take precedence; the world's wonders can seem a little hollow. Without the ability to share those moments with those closest to you, they somehow seem to lose a dimension. Conversely, when those you love are close at hand, the most routine destination can unlock a whole new vault of memories and shared experiences. Yes, a career in aviation has taken me to a world of wonderful places, but at some point the penny dropped and I truly appreciated that this life is about the people. Fortunately, I have been blessed with both and still ventured from Hall's Creek to Hollywood.

*****

39

The Ultimate Sacrifice

Where does the time go? Another anniversary of the space shuttle Challenger tragedy has passed. Few of us who were around at the time can forget the TV image of the conflagration and spiralling clouds of smoke lingering silently in the sky. The shocked faces looking skyward and the stilted commentary drowned in disbelief.

Yet sacrifice has always walked close beside the pursuit of new frontiers. Over the centuries, countless explorers and seaborne vessels failed to return as they sought the edge of the earth in search of new lands. Similarly, as the new realms of sky and space availed themselves, a new generation of pioneers put their lives on the line.

Otto Lilienthal, the great German aviation pioneer of the late nineteenth century set new benchmarks in the pursuit of manned flight with his gliders. Credited by the Wright brothers for his research, Lilienthal paid the ultimate price in 1896 when one of his gliders fell to earth. He was not the first and ultimately proved to be far from the last.

The early aviators were faced with huge adversity. Their machines were frail and the understanding of aerodynamics was in its infancy. Even as the technology of their machines developed over the decades, they still stretched their fledgling machines to the absolute limits of their performance and endurance. Shrinking the globe was a mammoth task and aviation wanted to accelerate the process. Air races, prize money, Government grants and celebrity were just some of the incentives, but the driving force ultimately came from within. Very few individuals would put their life on the line solely for material gain; the challenge was undoubtedly a prime motivator.

Yet time and again they perished trying. And these were not purely first time novices that history never even knew to forget, these were names established in the halls of aviation fame; Charles Kingsford Smith, Wiley Post, Amelia Earhart, Bert Hinkler, Bill Lancaster and Amy Johnson, to name but a handful. In one way or another, they perished in the very style in which they had lived their lives.

Their sacrifices have not been forgotten, nor did their losses answer all of the questions that aerospace was to ask of its people. As man sought to go higher, farther and faster, the boundaries were often pushed to breaking point and the human link was often the first to fold. Swept wings, jet engines, supersonic flight, pressurised hulls and the frontier of space continued to ask questions of the engineers, physicists and test pilots. Too often, it claimed many lives before an answer was ultimately found.

The great British aviation pioneer and designer, Sir Geoffrey DeHavilland, lost one of his sons while test flying a new generation jet aircraft, the DH108 Swallow. Another son died in a mid-air collision. The home of flight research in the United States, Edwards

Air Force Base, has seen more than its share of triumph and tragedy. It was home to the 'X-planes' and saw Chuck Yeager break the sound barrier in 1947. Neil Armstrong cut his teeth at Edwards on the likes of the X-15 before fate would ultimately determine that space was his destiny. Yet in the shadow of the advances loiters the losses and its streets bear the names of many of those heroes. Even the base is named after USAF test pilot, Glen Edwards, who perished with his crew testing the YB-49 'Flying Wing'.

It became apparent that the sky was not the limit and soon space became the new frontier. As the American Mercury astronauts were launched into orbit with increasing frequency, the Soviet Union was doing so with equal success in the 'space race'. Both sides encountered losses throughout this period of rapid technological advancement, including the horrific fireball of Apollo 1 on the launch pad during testing at Cape Canaveral. And while the brilliant failure of Apollo 13 was a very close call, the loss of the space shuttle Challenger in 1986 reminded us that space exploration is still a very dangerous business. The loss of Columbia on re-entry in 2003 re-affirmed the fact.

But for all the losses, ultimately the cause has advanced. In fact it has advanced at a pace that only the imagination would have dared to conjure a century ago. Within the span of an average human life, aviation developed from flimsy frames limping a few hundred feet to man standing upon the lunar surface. It is an achievement that all humanity can be proud of and has effectively made the world a smaller place. Its applications have been varied, from powerful war machines to vehicles of tremendous humanitarian aid and from craft of leisure to a means of rescue on cold, dark nights.

But as aviation continues forth, it is vital to remember those who have paid the ultimate price along the way, for it is their courage that has allowed this field of human endeavour to grow like no other. Their willingness to strap into confined cockpits and push the envelope has allowed the rest of the world to reap the benefits of air travel and aerospace in a far more relaxed and safer manner. In aviation, the safety of the masses has often been the achieved at a high cost to an individual.

Furthermore, the price of human life should serve to ward off complacency about forging new frontiers in the sky. It is not our natural realm; we are guests in the air above the earth. We should always pay due respect to our host, for the moment we don't, the skies have the potential to remind us of our lowly status in the most brutal manner.

So as we mark the 25th anniversary of the loss of 'Challenger', we should offer thanks to her crew and to all of those who have paid the ultimate price in pushing those boundaries in the sky. In tragedy we must always seek to find a greater purpose and learn from the past, so as to avoid history repeating itself. However, despite the lessons learnt, no loss will be the last as we move forward; unfortunately it is the price those heroes pay on our behalf. This cold reality has been with us since the beginning. As he lay on his death-bed the day after his fall to earth, the great Otto Lilienthal uttered, "Kleine Opfer müssen gebracht werden".................. "Small sacrifices must be made."

*****

40

Just one of those days....

It was just one of those days again.....in a good way.

Like so many mornings in the airline game it began in a hotel room with an alarm clock sounding at an hour too early to accurately recall. A shower, a shave and a stealthy exit, carefully trying not to slam the door and disturb the other guests. An exchange of pleasantries and a room key to the sole staff member manning the foyer desk, before a cheerful 'Good Morning' to my fellow pilot. As the car makes its way to the airport along the darkened roads, we both check the latest weather and radar paints on our new-age devices. What did we do before these things? In the briefing room we pore over the detailed weather and 'Notices to Airmen' before ordering our fuel load, passing through security and finally walking out to our aircraft sitting quietly on the tarmac.

The control tower was still asleep as we brought the Boeing to life for the day and then passengers started to climb aboard. A few more calculations and then the 'tower' was open for business. We received our 'airways clearance' from the chirpy Air Traffic Controller and I'm sure that I could smell coffee on his voice. The runway lights were on, the sun was threatening to rise in the east and we were all ready to go. Engines started; we're on our way.

Climbing out from Hobart, the darkness grew even deeper early in the flight as we entered a low layer of cloud. Some thousands of feet later the cloud began to glow and then I was in clear air with a line of bright orange sunrise back over my shoulder. The brilliance only lasted a few minutes, before once again the cloud consumed the aircraft and held it in its grasp until 30,000 feet. By then we had well and truly set course for Melbourne and a solid white blanket lay below us. Thirty minutes later and we were over Bass Strait with the thrust levers closing to initiate our descent into the Victorian capital.

Not much was happening on this sleepy Sunday morning, so air traffic control instructed us to fly a straight line at our maximum speed to join final approach for the northern runway; an instruction that we happily complied with. As the cloud thinned out the coastline lay below and we shadowed the waterline with the high-rise of the city looming ahead and to our right.

The view as we passed Melbourne's skyline was beautiful as we began to decelerate. The early morning sun silhouetted the buildings without affording the full detail of colour. But there was colour; seven or eight dots of colour. In the stillness of the early morning air, a sea of hot air balloons silently drifted into the sun's earliest rays and was illuminated by its light. Each periodically squeezed a burst of flame upwards from their gondola into the towering panelled teardrops above. Together they appeared to be untethered lanterns welcoming the day from on high. It was spectacular.

We continued on and landed at Melbourne, but after such a breathtaking start to the day, the latter phase of the flight could not compete as a spectacle. The flight deck truly is the best seat in the house and I treasure every day I spend there. Every day offers something new, so really, today was just another one of those days.....but in a good way.

*****

The Mustang

Refuelling the Tiger Moth. Old School.

41

One Tiger's Tale

At some point in my childhood, between converting Mum's clothes-horse to a P-51 Mustang and sitting atop our garage with binoculars, I asked my father a fairly simple question, "What was a Tiger Moth like?"

Starry-eyed, I awaited the reply that would define the sheer essence of aviation and the pioneer spirit. "The Tiger?" he started, "It was cold, draughty, noisy and you'd end up with windburn, sunburn and goggle marks to prove it" He tapped his empty pipe on the veranda. Paused. Then continued, "…but it was blessed good trainer for its day. It taught you to use your feet. It taught you a lot of things." That answer was about as extensive as Dad would ever venture when it came to reminiscences, however, if it was a technical question you'd be best advised to take a seat with a pen at the ready. Nevertheless, I think this is when the first seeds of owning an antique aeroplane were probably sown.

I was surrounded by aviation growing up. Dad had first started flying privately at Wagga Wagga NSW in 1948, whilst an apprentice mechanic in the RAAF. His early flying with Eric Condon lasted about six months before he was mustered for aircrew and posted to Point Cook. His subsequent career saw active service in Korea with 77 Squadron, the early days of the 'Connie' traversing the globe, primitive attempts at cloud-seeding, umpteen hours of instructing, testing and checking before winding up his career with the NSW Air Ambulance in 1986. Even after this he used to "do a bit" with Rebel Air and Schofields. As a youngster, I took every opportunity to tag along to the airport and not infrequently buckle up beside Dad. I vividly remember old Syd Marshall and his collection of aircraft at Bankstown and sitting in the Mustangs that Dad had flown at a previous time. Even today, I treasure an old Hurricane model Syd gave me. The older aircraft had always been of more interest to me. Their shape. Their character. Their history.

In 1994 I was fortunate to be given a relatively rewarding and seemingly secure job with the now-defunct Ansett Airlines, (enough said). I had no sooner "checked to line" than I noticed a Tiger Moth restoration project for sale. I made the initial enquiries, but questions hovered over the completeness of the aircraft and the logistics of an interstate restoration daunted me. I let this opportunity slide; nevertheless, it was effectively the turning point for my childhood dream. I started reading everything I could get my hands on and chasing up information from any source available, particularly the living, breathing kind. I found loitering around fly-ins to be particularly beneficial and the friendliness and generosity (i.e. free rides) of those involved with antique aviation bolstered my decision to go ahead if I could fund the project adequately. My wife agreed.

In 1996 my wife was fortunate to be given a relatively rewarding and secure job in aviation, (fingers-crossed).

Together we ventured to a place we had heard about and flown over numerous times; Luskintyre. Nestled in the Hunter Valley, just west of Maitland, lies a facility busily putting long-forgotten deHavillands back in the air. My first memory of Ray Windred's hangar was its' similarity to Santa's workshop. There were numerous tradesmen at different stations, each thoroughly engrossed in a task that seemed to call for patience as the primary tool. Access was gained by weaving between airframes, some standing proudly on their own undercart, others braced in jigs ready for covering. My wife and I did the "cook's tour" of the restorations and the surrounding airfield. We subsequently retired to one of the vineyards for lunch, where we agreed no decisions would be made on grounds of diminished responsibility.

Time passed as we attended to other minor matters such as buying and selling a home, but as 1997 drew to a close we advised Ray Windred that we would purchase one of his old airframes and have him restore it to its previous glory. This was to be Ray's eighteenth rebuild of the type. One of the factors that made purchasing an antique aircraft more attractive was the history that is attached to these aircraft of yesteryear. Accordingly, we set about finding the history of our airframe, construction No. 82358. In the process, we made contact with pilots that had flown in the aircraft in its war service and a number of these gentlemen kindly forwarded copies of their log books. Together with old RAAF documents and photos of the restoration taking place, my wife and I compiled a journal relating to our project. This exercise is one which I would highly recommend as it keeps the spirits up through those delays, trials and tribulations that are associated with the rebuild of an old aeroplane. And on completion it serves to tell a fascinating tale.

The aircraft had an interesting history. To the best of my knowledge, it was built at Hatfield in the United Kingdom as part of the original order 0I758 that saw the British Air Ministry deliver 100 Tiger Moths to the RAAF. Arriving at RAAF Richmond in February 1940, it subsequently served with a variety training units throughout the war, maintaining its British markings of N9257 throughout. "De-mobbed" at Cunderdin, W.A. in 1947, it began its' civilian life under the markings VH-AKN, passing from private hands to a crop-dusting operation in April 1955. As was the way, the front cockpit was gutted and replaced with a hopper for spraying. This commercial chapter of 82358 was to be short-lived, crashing at Midland Junction, W.A. eight weeks later.

Almost 46 years to the day of its crash, on June 12th 2001, the Tiger again took to the air at Luskintyre. Restored in a civil scheme, with a new call-sign, I finally got my hands on my childhood dream. The euphoria of the flight that followed very closely rivalled my first solo twenty years before.............it was great. The only regret? That the 'old man' wasn't there to see it. I did a number of flights at Luskintyre to consolidate my own familiarity with the aeroplane and monitor the engine and airframe for any gremlins that may surface. The aircraft performed without fault and after a "5 hour check-up" I prepared to ferry VH-ZUP to its' new home.

As I was delayed by early morning Hunter Valley fog, my wife set out ahead in our car with the plan being to rendezvous outside the hangar at our home airfield. Late morning, I became airborne and armed merely with an antiquated P8 compass, I set course to the south. There wasn't a cloud in the sky and I took every opportunity to sightsee as I learned lesson after lesson of navigating in an open cockpit. Midway I discovered that sitting on one's charts was far more satisfactory than the clipboard I had earlier employed and that recovering one's pencil from beneath the many layers of clothing was easier said than done. All this and no autopilot! I laughed at myself and took absolute pleasure in stumbling through the grassroots of aviation.

As I trekked further south into a very light headwind I calculated that the aircraft was making good time.......for a Tiger Moth. Even so, the freeway traffic seemed to be making a very comparable pace until the benefit of straight-line travel opened up a lead for me. My wife, having stopped to pick up my Mum, a former air force radar operator, saw me pass overhead, consequently on my arrival at Mittagong the welcoming party was yet to arrive. As you would expect, I took the opportunity to waste time over the beautiful Southern Highlands and the hamlet of Bowral, home of Sir Donald Bradman. It is a great privilege to be able to simply wander about the sky.

The ground party finally caught up and I was out of excuses to remain aloft. Touching down on Runway 24, I rolled out to the hangar that is now home to this Tiger. An old Royal Aero Club mate and his wife were there so we took to the air for a quick hop, as you're prone to do. Back on the ground, I was all out of excuses and daylight, so we pushed the aircraft into the hangar for the night. Armed with champagne we toasted the Tiger and even allowed a little to trickle down the propeller. All in all, the flight had been cold, noisy and draughty and I did indeed bear windburn and goggle marks, but there was no doubt, this Tiger Moth was a blessed good aeroplane.

*****

42

The Pioneers

Seven years after the Wright Brothers first crept into the skies, powered flight came to Australia in 1910. The States had been united under Federation for less than a decade and the population was just over four million, yet this fledgling nation was set to make its mark in the brave new world of aviation. Within that four million there were some who were at the forefront of aviation's brave new world.

Before powered flight took wings, Lawrence Hargrave had been Australia's original aviation pioneer. Edging himself aloft whilst attached to a series of box-kites, his research unlocked a number of the mysteries of flight. Always the scientist rather than the entrepreneur, Hargraves published his findings freely and contributed greatly to the advancement of aviation around the world. In fact, the Voisin brothers of France credited Hargraves for much of their ultimate success in aircraft design.

When powered flight was first achieved at Digger's Rest in Victoria on March 18th 1910, it was a Voisin aeroplane that carried the pilot aloft. Incredibly, the pilot that day was the famous American magician and escape artist, Harry Houdini. This was the first 'recorded' controlled powered flight in Australia, though conjecture has raged for literally a century. Just as the Wright Brothers were reportedly beaten to the punch by New Zealander, Richard Pearse, Houdini had no shortage of challengers for the title. Colin Defries, George Taylor and Fred Custance were all named as possible predecessors, but history has recorded Houdini's flight at Plumpton's Paddock as the first. Much like current day athletic records, there may have been faster times achieved but without official ratification the record will not stand. In Houdini's case, he was the first to have signed witness accounts and critically, an image of the aircraft in flight.

While kudos may flow from being the first, it is the fact that so many pioneering aviators were pushing to be first that resulted in the progress that was made. The fact is that they all contributed in their own way to Australia's dawn of aviation. However, for the nation, the major stride came on July 16th when an Australian, John Duigan took flight for the first time in an Australian aircraft. Also taking place in Victoria at Mia Mia, the feat was particularly noteworthy as Duigan and his brother had designed the aircraft with very little technical guidance other than text books and magazines from overseas. Mighty oaks from little acorns grow and Australian aviation was well on its way.

From frail machines making short hops and uneasy circuits, aviation advanced with a flurry initiated by the Great War of 1914-1918. Just as would occur twenty years later during the second global conflict, the teeth of the war machine evolved aircraft technologically at a rate that could only be imagined in peace-time. From branches of the Army, Air Forces took root along with the Naval Air Service and these gave birth to a new generation of advanced aviators. From their ranks the names of the Smith Brothers, Bert Hinkler and Charles Kingsford Smith emerged.

Following the war's end, Australian Prime Minister "Billy" Hughes announced a prize of £10,000 for the first Australians to fly from England to Australia in less than 30 days. A decorated WW1 pilot, Captain Ross Smith joined with his brother Lieutenant Keith Smith and Sergeants Bennett and Shiers to compete for the prize. Smith had served with the fledgling Australian Flying Corps (AFC) and accrued a relatively significant amount of experience on multi-engine bombers. Using a former bomber, a Vickers Vimy, the crew battled atrocious weather and a series of mishaps to land in Darwin on December 10th 1919, after 28 days and more than 11,000 miles. Both brothers received knighthoods while their non-commissioned crew were made officers and their Vickers Vimy still resides today in their home state at Adelaide Airport.

Whilst the Smith brothers and their crew succeeded, another Australian had been unable to enter the race with a little Sopwith Dove and continued to dream of flying to his homeland; he was Bert Hinkler. Lieutenant Hinkler had served with the Royal Naval Air Service (RNAS) during World War One and had also been decorated. However, his fascination with flight pre-dated the conflict and as a boy he had studied the Ibis and made successful glider flights on the dunes near his home in Bundaberg. After serving post-war as a test pilot with the Avro Company, Hinkler finally made his flight to Australia in 1928, solo in a tiny Avro Avian in only fifteen days. He went onto achieve a number of feats, but none more significant and more overlooked than his 1931 flight from Canada to South America, across the South Atlantic to Africa and onto London in a DH Puss Moth. Always tending to avoid the spotlight, Hinkler tragically died in 1933 on a hillside in the Tuscan Mountains of Italy in undertaking yet another brave solo attempt.

As a pilot with the Royal Flying Corps (RFC), Charles Kingsford Smith had been both decorated and wounded, losing part of his left foot. After the war, "Smithy" had flown commercially in operations ranging from barnstorming to some of the first airline services. However, he will forever be remembered for his mammoth Trans-Pacific flight in 1928 in his aircraft, the "Southern Cross". Along with Charles Ulm and two Americans, James Warner and Harry Lyon, the four men traversed the world's largest water mass and more than 7,000 miles. Flying through challenging weather with minimal navigation aids to assist, the "Southern Cross" provided a deafening backdrop, where communication between the crew was achieved by passing notes. On arriving at Brisbane's Eagle Farm Airport, the Fokker Tri-Motor was swamped by a huge crowd and Smithy was catapulted into the limelight.

The subsequent years saw a series of record-breaking flights, high drama and the occasional scandal. Along with Ulm, he founded Australian National Airways in 1929, but their dream perished in 1931 following the loss of two aircraft; the "Southern Cloud" and the "Southern Sun". With the Great Depression filling the headlines, Smithy continued to undertake aviation exploits and adventures, though his beloved "Southern Cross" was ultimately retired in 1935. This followed an aborted Trans-Tasman attempt that saw oil transferred between engines by P.G. Taylor and John Stannage climbing out onto the wing. Chasing the Australia to England speed record in November of the same year, Smithy and his co-pilot Tommy Pethybridge went missing near Burma, with an undercarriage leg washing up on Aye Island the only trace found to this day.

The Australian girls were not to be outdone either. In the 1930s aviatrix Lores Bonney was setting her own aviation records when female pilots were few and far between. Inspired by Bert Hinkler, Bonney began breaking records for women pilots in 1931 and went onto achieve her gender's first flights around Australia, from Australia to England and Australia to South Africa. She was planning to fly around the world when World War Two intervened. In a world that remembers Amy Johnson and immortalises Amelia Earhart, Lores Bonney is relatively unknown. Although unlike Johnson, Earhart and numerous other contemporary aviation pioneers, Lores Bonney survived to 96 years of age, passing away at her Queensland home in 1994.

So how did such a young, small nation produce so many pioneers in the early development of aviation? Many have alluded to the resilience and initiative of the Australian character of that bygone era. Resourcefulness was a prerequisite to survival in settling such a harsh interior and this is often seen as a character trait that translated well into the new frontier of flight.

For some the answer lies in World War One. Accomplished horsemen were perceived as ideal potential aviators and Australia was rich in men meeting this profile. As a result, many were subsequently recruited into the Royal Flying Corps from which the Australian Flying Corps ultimately grew. This grounding provided a relatively high ratio of Australians with a thirst for the skies.

Perhaps it was simply the tyranny of distance. Cast off thousands of miles from Mother England, Australians of that era had much closer ties to the motherland and monarchy. Aviation offered an ideal means to enhance communication across the empire, while also offering a means by which to traverse their own vast brown land. The skies offered speeds that could not be challenged by sea-faring vessels or horse drawn coaches. Then, as now, Australia's geography dictated that it was a nation best served by aviation.

A combination of all of these factors consequently determined Australian aviation's role on the world stage. There is no doubting that for its size, the island continent fought well above its weight. As pioneers were replaced by regular air services and nations grew closer through technology, Australia continued to play leading roles in aviation and aerospace, though often these achievements were not as headline grabbing as Smithy and Hinkler. However Dr. David Warren's development of the Flight Data Recorder (FDR) in the 1950s was no less spectacular.

Aviation will always be central to Australian culture as long as the miles separate its citizens. The leather helmets, goggles and open cockpits may have given way to faster jets and flight levels, but the ties that bind still remain. As a nation much has been achieved in the last hundred years, though undoubtedly aviation can be held up as the poster boy of 20th century evolution. As the 21st century gets underway and the global economies dictate that business and progress further diminish borders, only a crystal ball could perceive where Australia and aviation will travel in the next century. What is for sure is that our debt to the pioneers will always remain.

*****

43

We apologise for the delay, however.........

"We apologise for the delay, however.........." How many flights have started with that phrase coming from the flight deck even before the engines have begun to spin over? Furthermore, the length of the pause that occurs after the word "however...." is generally proportionate to the length of the delay. Meanwhile in the cabin, the announcement is met with a collective sigh and a ferocious amount of 'thumb dynamics' as text messages are fired off to waiting friends and family.

And yet while the delay is the all too frequent curse of modern air travel, it is worth sparing a thought for just why that delay may be taking place. The obvious offenders spring to mind, such as the small technical fault. Often easily rectified, the administration required to re-certify the aircraft documentation can absorb as many minutes as the actual maintenance procedure. But let's consider the alternative course of action. The pilots could ignore the symptoms of a possible fault and depart with some aspect of the aeroplane under suspicion. Not only is this unsafe, but the sheer fact that any issue that could be rectified on the ground is left unresolved would undoubtedly play on the mind of any self-respecting pilot in the air. This distraction is far from ideal. So when the clock ticks over while a technical issue is resolved, feel free to sigh and text message as desired, but be thankful that you're sitting in an aircraft of an airline that won't accept 'near enough' as 'good enough'. There are some airlines around the world that just might.

Beyond the technical fault, there is the 'connecting passenger' issue. Often fellow passengers have transited the globe and along the way they have had to clear Customs twice and quite possibly cross the dateline. That final domestic sector may see them home to loved ones after a draining 24 hours of international travel. Conversely, an onward connection to an international flight may also see a few minutes delay making literally a world of difference to family destined for distant lands. This world can be selfless enough these days, so the trade off of a few minutes to assist a fatigued fellow traveller isn't really a price too great to pay. It may be inconvenient and frustrating, but put yourself in their shoes for the day may come when a flight holds off departing to assist you. Remember, we're all in this together.

Let's not forget the crew ether. Pilots and flight attendants also have lives beyond the fuselage that are often disrupted by delays and changes. Public holidays and weekends, dinners and birthdays often fall victim to not only anticipated rostering but last minute changes. Granted, these conditions come with the territory and every crew member takes on the profession understanding that this is the job. However, what is not often appreciated is that crew will frequently extend their tour of duty, overnight without notice or a change of clothes, or come into work on a rostered day off rather than see the airline and its passengers disrupted any further. Fortunately, there is still a high level of professional integrity in commercial aviation and it is one of the joys of being employed within the industry. So when you're seated, waiting to go and a faceless, uniformed being flashes past into the flight deck, bear in mind that they might not be running late. They may have left a child's birthday party or ballet recital to ensure that a couple of hundred strangers can attend theirs.

In fact, the co-ordination required for an on-time departure is an exercise in choreography that would do any dance company proud. From crew, fuel and catering to maintenance, flight planning and baggage, everything runs to a precise schedule. Interdependent and time critical, each component relies upon the punctuality of the other to ensure a harmonious conclusion and subsequent on-time departure. In turn, each aircraft has to share these ground resources with other aircraft in an act of co-operation that would impress the United Nations. If a time lapse camera could capture all the people, machines and paperwork that needs to occur to keep an airline fleet moving, the resulting film may well make a community of worker ants look like they're on a holiday in the Maldives.

Every person in that finely balanced chain is sensitive to the impact of delays upon their valued customers and tries their utmost to achieve the planned time of departure. Yet their responsibility extends far beyond the ticking clock and they must always ensure that the task is completed thoroughly and safely. (Rushing has a very bad name in the corridors of air safety departments). And even when the brakes are released on time and the flight begins as anticipated, a new set of potential delays surface through subtleties of air traffic control, weather, runway configuration and airport congestion. Honestly, rather than lamenting the delays, it is often worth pondering the high rate at which this complex sequence of events successfully comes together.

As always, safety must come first in aviation. Combining safety with efficiency is the ultimate benchmark for any organisation that seeks to call the skies its office. And for any aircraft to meet its schedule, a mass of dedicated individuals each must play their part in conjunction with many others in a way that is absolutely invisible to the passengers. Despite their best efforts, sometimes the plan may miss its mark and departure time comes and goes without success. Next time this occurs spare a thought for those unseen folks that are trying their utmost to see that flight depart in the safest possible manner. The cause may be beyond their control, but they will still seek to find a way to overcome the challenge and still turn their cog over in this complex, time-critical sequence. And should a solution still be some time in coming.............."We apologise for this delay, however.............."

*****

44

One Night Over Europe

It's 4am and I'm writing. The pre-dawn hours are always the quietest and friendliest to put my thoughts into words. Similarly, these wee hours are often the busiest for long-haul flight crews around the world as their destination draws closer. The aircraft galley begins to stir as the cabin crew ready breakfast for the sleeping passengers, while the flight crew begins to gather the latest weather and enter an 'arrival' into the Flight Management Computer. The long hours of darkness that have passed are now building towards the final, high workload hour of the flight and a safe arrival for the hundreds of people on board.

The smell of coffee pervades the flight deck and the balance of the crew leave their bunks to join the pilots 'on watch' as all hands must be on deck for the final stage of the journey. The glow of city lights below offer up a luminous atlas for orientation and those reliable engines continue to hum, just as they have for hour after hour through the night. This very scene is being enacted on board numerous airliners around the world as I tap the keyboard in the solitude of my 'study' and I recall one of the first nights I experienced that scene myself.

After a night in Bangkok, we had weaved our way over the Bay of Bengal, beyond India, Pakistan and onto Afghanistan. Yes, Afghanistan, where military air traffic was displayed as anonymous blips on the flight panel and 'Boss Man' radioed through our clearance from his position overhead, granting us safe passage through the airspace over Kabul. Over Eastern Europe the scratchy transmissions of HF radio had given way to the clearer tones of VHF, although the deep, broad accents still made comprehension difficult, even if the reception was clear. For a boy from the suburbs of Sydney with a lifetime of flying within the Australian coastlines, it was brave new world; but one that I found fascinating.

All through the night I had tracked our progress in an old atlas, progressively moving a small adhesive red arrow along the page. Aside from a tremendous means of orientation, I found that the atlas brought the journey alive in a way that the moving triangle and magenta line of the 'Navigation Display' just couldn't manage. Despite cruising in the darkness, the terrain below seemed to come alive from the coloured topographical maps and the smaller cities which may have lacked any aeronautical significance were often rich in other ways. As my index finger pushed along the page and over borders, I was a student in history and geography as well as a pilot.

But it was as I approached Western Europe that first time that my interest was truly peaked. The nations that had filled my text-books and imagination as a lad were now beginning to slip under the nose of the Boeing 747. Germany, the Netherlands, Belgium and France seemed as though you could throw a net over them and yet it is hard to imagine cramming their combined history into a galaxy, let alone such a small patch of earth. To the west a dark strip appeared and the absence of light was no doubt the English Channel where armadas had once sailed and furious battles aloft had seen Spitfires and Messerschmitts clash. Dawn was still a little way off as the Thames appeared, weaving through the densely lit city of London as we lined up to land at Heathrow.

As the air traffic controller unhurriedly spoke to a multitude of aeroplanes, we began to extend flap and lower the landing gear to comply with speed restrictions and ready the aircraft for landing. All the while the wonders of automation steered the course and allowed the crew the brain-space to manage the giant Boeing through its final, busy moments of flight before disengaging the autopilot and rejoining the earth.

That night in London as the joys of jet-lag had me staring at the ceiling in lieu of tedious infomercials, I relived that final hour of flight and the amazing descent into England. I would prop up on one elbow and flick through the atlas, before laying back down and piecing together the flightpath and its historical tale. But there was something more, this very route had been flown so very differently years before. As I recalled the glow of our flight panel and its colourful, informative displays, the warmth of the flight deck and the convenience of the coffee cup holders, I thought of young men who never knew such luxury.

These were the crews of Bomber Command in World War Two. Freezing in their deafening Lancasters, Halifaxes, Wellingtons and the like, the sight of the Thames would have meant so very much more. It was the first hint that they might have just defied the odds and survived the night. Even so, their aircraft may have been limping home, battle damaged after the crossed beams of search-lights had caught them and the anti-aircraft brutalised them. Some of the crew may have been bandaged and bleeding, praying for the moment when the wheels again touched down on the soil of Mother England between the blazing paths that lit the runway's edge.

They may well have not seen the Thames or the blacked out city of London, hidden beneath a low cover of English stratus. Feeling their way back home, edging down foot by foot until their base, or any suitable airfield offered them salvation. There was no galley stirring with crew, or omelettes on the hot plate for these young men and I felt a pang of guilt and indebtedness as I recalled the comfortable surroundings of my flight. They were so very young, with a man in his mid-twenties almost qualifying as an old man. At an age when I was concerned about playing sport and Friday night revelry, these young men were sacrificing their tomorrows. Mere boys at the helm of lumbering machines, launching into the darkened war-torn skies with a poor chance of ever making it back. Those in Bomber Command had a loss rate of over 40 per cent and more than 50,000 young men never came home. One of those was a family friend; Bob Eggins.

I continued to be in awe of that descent into London for my remaining time in international operations. It is truly a remarkable experience to watch such a significant portion of our planet unfold before you. However, my wonder was subsequently tinged with a different kind of awe and a great deal of respect after that sleepless night in a South Kensington hotel room. Each time I would take a moment to remember those who had gone before and those who had fallen, for my remarkable journey has only been possible by virtue of their ultimate sacrifice one night over Europe.

In Memory of
Flying Officer Robert Bruce Eggins
467 Squadron RAAF
Killed in Action 4th March 1945
Aged 20.
Lest We Forget.

*****

45

Lighting Up the Night

The four engines hummed hypnotically through night sky over the Pacific. While Honolulu sat only a matter of miles away, the passengers on board the Boeing 747 were blissfully unaware, curled up beneath their blankets in the darkened cabin. The cabin crew chatted in hushed tones behind the galley's heavy curtains, planning their shopping strategy when they arrived in San Francisco in a few hours time.

On the flight deck the tone was also hushed so as not to disturb the resting crew at the compartment's rear. The aircraft continued to track faultlessly along the magenta line on the instrument flight display as the 'Top of Descent' indicator and San Francisco edged ever closer down the screen. I called up the latest weather reports through the aircraft's onboard system and shared them with my fellow pilot. It was set to be a beautiful day, but we ran through all of our available options and fuel status to ensure that all our bases were covered.

The first rays of the sun had not yet crept above the horizon but a portion of the upper atmosphere was just revealing the first traces of the new day. A light, faint haze met the curved shadow of the earth's outline in an arc that spanned the horizon from left to right. The day was encroaching on the stratosphere, but not yet on the earth below.

The first indication that something special was taking place was not visual in nature. It was the chatter of American crews transiting the busy route between the mainland and Hawaii. "Can you see that?", "What is it?" and "Is someone starting World War Three?" The exchanges peaked my interest, but gave no indication of the location or nature of the commotion. Then there was a hint. "There. On the horizon. Down low. It's brilliant!"

I leaned forward in my seat and peered into the darkness below. Nothing. Resting my arms on the top of the instrument panel, I cupped my eyes with my hands to keep the glow of the instrument panel to a minimum. Then I saw it. A tiny, bright intense light, like the tip of a white hot arc welder. Almost stationary, it was growing larger, ever so slightly. Seemingly in a matter of seconds it grew from a needle point to a distinct flame, growing both in mass and momentum at a rate that was difficult to comprehend.

"What is it?" the other pilot echoed my thoughts, equally astounded. Still it grew each and every second to a brighter and more impressive light, seemingly darting skyward. There was no perspective available to gauge distance or offer an idea of its size; just an ever-increasing intensity. Then someone identified the UFO that was captivating every crew aloft that night. "It's a launch out of Vandenberg."

A rocket launch from the US Air Force base on the west coast. Now everything made sense. It was hundreds of miles away, but so powerful that it was clearly seen by every aircraft in the flight levels and as it climbed it seemed to grow in speed as its trajectory could now be viewed in profile. Up through the darkness and onwards towards the illuminated upper atmosphere, the rocket would reach the daylight before the night's end for any of the citizens below. In an absolutely spectacular display of sheer energy, the projectile closed in on the arc between night and day, dark and light. One almost expected it to tear through some barrier between dawn like ripping fabric. And then it virtually did.

Just as its furious flightpath penetrated the arc.

Wooomf!

A flash of light that seemingly lit up the night for an instant before a mammoth expanding ring of vapour exploded across the sky. Like those TV documentaries that show the final burst of light across the galaxy from a dying star, such was the scope of this amazing sight. In reality it was the rocket jettisoning a stage of its cylindrical being to leave the 'sharp end' to continue its journey into 'earth orbit'. Bound for space and relieved of much of its load, the remaining portion seemed to accelerate ever-faster and ever-higher. I craned my neck to look skyward and follow the lone beacon as it roared away and finally faded from my mere mortal sight.

Wow!

It had departed as quickly as it had emerged. All that now remained was the ring across the horizon which was now merging with the moisture to develop into a cloud system of its own, like an atmospheric calling card. Its passage had been silent, but its impact was immense.

Over the years, I have been very fortunate to see many wonderful sights from this treasured vantage point in the sky, but that pre-dawn morning off the west coast of the United States will always rank very highly. In a matter of minutes, a simple light had transformed the sky and left everyone who had witnessed it breathless.

Meanwhile, the four engines of the 747 still continued to hum hypnotically and the cabin crew chatted while the passengers slept, blissfully unaware. But for this boy from Sydney, Australia, I would never look at the night sky quite the same again.

*****

Squadron Leader Kenneth McGlashan's Hawker Hurricane on the beach at Dunkirk then and in 1988. (Images: via D. McGlashan)

46

A Veteran's Tale

Along the way we all have cause to encounter many different personalities; some interesting, some complicated and others that spring to mind for all of the wrong reasons. They can be found in a marketplace in some far-away hidden corner of the globe, or right around the corner next to the pie shop. Part of the fun is that you never know where you'll find them.

Some time back, I took to speaking to veteran aircrew of past conflicts in an effort to record their stories. It allowed me to tie together my interest in history, writing and aviation. Along the way meeting real characters who have 'been there and done that', yet still retain their modesty and the art of the understatement. While some stories are published, others are simply retained by the family to pass on to the enquiring grandchildren, whose questions always seem to surface around ANZAC and Memorial Day assignment time.

Two years ago, I was approached by one such survivor of World War Two. Not through the Department of Veteran's Affairs, or the

Returned Servicemen's League, but an electrician. Repairing all and sundry in the aftermath of a lightning strike, the 'sparky' mentioned an old fellow he knew who had been trying to get his story recorded for a few years. He'd started to write it himself, but hadn't gotten very far; maybe I'd like to have a chat with him?

Kenneth Butterworth McGlashan was standing in his shed, shaking his head at a recalcitrant lathe when I first met him. He'd taken to restoring tired antique furniture in his retirement and his workshop was a mix of turned table legs and sawdust. Turning away from his tools, Kenneth greeted me warmly and immediately began chatting about his Royal Air Force days. With a Scottish accent and no hesitation, the 84 year-old started to describe an aerial combat over Dunkirk in 1940 on which he had come out on the wrong side. We wandered inside and began to chat over a cup of tea about aerial campaigns that had become folklore; the Battle of Britain, Dieppe and D-Day. Kenneth had been there for all of them as a fighter pilot, he was one of 'The Few' who had defended Britain in her darkest hour.

His sharp eyes hadn't aged a day, nor had his sense of humour. He related anecdote after anecdote with tremendous clarity and the hours ticked by until it was time for me to leave. Sensing my movement toward the door, Kenneth asked me if I was interested in writing his story and I knew I was, however I knew that this wasn't a magazine article or a short story for the family archives; it was a book. This bloke had received his wings on rag and tube biplanes before the war and flown through the entire conflict, from the retreat at Dunkirk to the landings at Normandy and beyond. He was living history and I was hooked. I had to say yes.

Was I up to writing such a book? Between a two year-old, a wife pregnant with twins and good dose of self-doubt, I had reservations. But as I sat in Kenneth's lounge room a week later with the wheels of a tape recorder slowly turning, I started to gather momentum. Not through any skill on my part, but because Kenneth was a natural story teller with an 'A Grade' memory. He jumped from episode to episode, but I let him go as sorting out the chronology was my job. For a starting point, I couldn't go past the tale of Dunkirk with which he had first captivated me.

He had been nineteen years of age as he sat perched above the English Channel in his new single-engined Hawker Hurricane. The airframe had only eight hours in the air and, by modern standards, Kenneth didn't have much more. Leading the rear section of three at 25,000 feet, he was tasked with covering the backs of his leading sections. Not long over the Channel, one of his trio turned back with engine trouble, leaving him and Geoff Howitt to fly as a pair. As they flew toward the plume of smoke lifting skyward from Dunkirk on the French coast, the massive evacuation of allied troops was taking place on the waves below in everything from Thames paddle-steamers to personal yachts.

Suddenly, the leading sections dived towards a flock of marauding German bombers. Simultaneously an ear piercing squeal rang out in Kenneth's headsets and his wingman broke formation clean in front of him as a pair of Messerschmitts roared from left to right. McGlashan rolled in on his foe, but seconds later heard what sounded like an alarm clock going off behind his head. (It was actually bullets hitting the armour-plating.) Reality struck when the port side of his Hurricane began ripping apart under a hail of gunfire and red tracers skipped between his legs, tearing up the piping and framework of his aeroplane's floor.

What ensued was a turbulent spinning plummet towards the French coast. When the attack abated, he attempted to level out and bale out as he knew that his fighter was bleeding to death. Crippled, the Hurricane was attacked again and he was ultimately forced down on the beach just south of the Belgian border. On the ground, he hurried from his fighter and dived beneath one of a sea of abandoned trucks on the beach. His subsequent nine mile walk to Dunkirk was a drama that included being shot at by German infantry and being threatened at bayonet-point by French Algerians, but ultimately it was a walk of isolation. As a nineteen year old he watched Spitfires crash into the sea and dead soldiery adrift on the swell like so much flotsam as he trudged toward the final point on the Continent held by allied forces.

Needless to say, Ken survived his encounter over Dunkirk. After an eventful boat ride back to England he went on to fly in the Battle of Britain from the RAF's easternmost airfield at Hawkinge until it was abandoned and laid to waste by the Luftwaffe. At this time his squadron was transferred to Ireland, where they trained foreign pilots on the Hurricane and attempted to protect coastal towns and the vital shipping routes supplying the British Isles from the west. There was no radar or organised control system in this region, so it was not unusual for the pilots to be scrambled by an irate Postmaster yelling down the phone, "We're being attacked! What are you going to do about it?"

From Ireland he would be a pioneer in night-fighting in a time when pilots were force fed carrots to improve their night vision. Stacked from 13,000 feet at 500 foot intervals above a burning Merseyside, the 'advanced' technique of detection was to wait for the bombers silhouettes to appear against the backdrop of the inferno. The fighters would then dive down, but inherently the bombers had already slipped away into the veil of darkness. Later in the war he would 'night fight' again, this time in company with a bomber equipped with a massive light in its nose. Termed 'Turbinlite', this technique involved sneaking up on the target in absolute darkness before illuminating it with a 2,700 million candlepower searchlight. This highly unsuccessful game of cat and mouse provided a greater risk to friend through collision than to foe through combat.

Through the disastrous raid on Dieppe in which Kenneth's aircraft was again badly shot up, he continued to fly operationally. On the eve of D-Day, he was one of a handful of aircraft airborne in darkness over France seeking out the German aircraft designed to jam the communications of the Normandy landings. Following D-Day he was deemed 'Tour Expired' and was to be pulled from operational flying. Instead he was seconded to BOAC and sent to Cairo as the British carrier set about re-establishing civil air routes in the Middle East. Be it serving in Cyprus through the EOKA campaign, welcoming in the jet age in Gloster Meteors and de Havilland Vampires or winning the Air Force Cross, there always seemed to be something happening for Kenneth McGlashan.

He finally retired from the RAF in 1958 and later established his family and a civilian life in Australia. In 1990 he received a very cryptic letter from the Tangmere Aviation Museum who was undertaking some research following the discovery of the Hawker Hurricane that Kenneth had left on the Dunkirk beach in 1940. Today, that aircraft is readying to take to the English skies once more.

So tale after tale occupied afternoon after afternoon. I would sit and listen as Kenneth would detail his extraordinary life and story of survival, taping every word before spending the night tying it together into some sort of order. Slowly but surely, his life became the book we had both envisaged. We agreed to title it in a manner that reflected Kenneth's level-headed approach and made a humourous jibe at the fact he had a few RAF aircraft make 'unscheduled' landings in his time. "Down to Earth" seemed very appropriate.

Along the way, I gained two valuable friends in Kenneth and his wife, Doreen and this is another wonderful by-product of my hobby. Sadly, when the book was launched at Kenneth's old stomping grounds during the UK's Duxford Air Show, he had not lived to see it happen. However, Doreen made the long trip to the England to be a part of the event. On the second day of the air show she was flown by helicopter to be reunited with the restoration of Kenneth's Hurricane. In her nineties, Doreen is insistent that she'll be back to see the fighter fly once more.

Kenneth always stressed that by numbers, there were three thousand fighter pilots who defended the realm through the Battle of Britain and within this sum only 3 per cent were officially recognised as "Aces". He was always proud to be counted amongst the remaining 97 per cent To me this in many ways sums up who he was.

His life was an extraordinary tale. I didn't have to venture to some far flung corner to find it though; Kenneth McGlashan was virtually over my back fence and my life became richer because of it.

*****

47

A Place to Land

Another airfield is under threat. This time a mobile phone tower is planned for erection within the immediate vicinity of a long established airfield whose roots date back to the dark days of World War Two. In a scene that is being played out globally, land developers, noise-sensitive neighbours and all manner of parties are eyeing off those parcels of land that aeroplanes call home.

While curfews, noise abatement procedures and movement caps exert their own form of pressure upon major aviation hubs, it is the smaller general aviation airfields that are feeling the pinch to the point of extinction. These sites are seen as valuable tracts of land just awaiting development. Often close to infrastructure, transport and growing city centres, developers see the airfields as a jackpot waiting to happen. Originally they sat at a socially acceptable distance from the populous, but the cities have grown to encroach upon their space and now object to their presence. The neighbours protest against the noise footprint and the chance of an aircraft crashing through their roof, while decibels and death are far more forthcoming from other means in this life. Airports just seem to be an easy target.

So when did aviation become so annoying to the greater community? At what point did they move from hoisting Lindbergh onto their shoulders and begin cursing those confounded machines? As with so many things, familiarity ended up breeding a degree of contempt. The benefits of air transport became an expectation and a right, rather than the source of fascination and admiration they once had been. For those who indulged in the pursuit of aviation in anything other than the most mandatory form, an air of elitism also began to alienate the greater community. While any general aviation exponent will point out the truth behind this myth, we only have to look as far as the television to realise that the story is not always portrayed with precision. Perception becomes reality.

So what is the answer as another airstrip is graded under? Aviation has by design continued to make aviation more neighbourly with quieter and greener technology and flightpaths that minimise the impact on those who reside near airfields. However in aviation, ultimately what goes up must come down and vice versa. Thrust can be managed, circuit directions changed and hours of operation restricted, but at some point aviation will generate noise and the land developers are only too happy to highlight this as they cast their eyes on the prize.

The defence of "we were here first" is also ringing hollow as many historic airfields are going asunder. Just look at the famous Meigs Field in Chicago which was quite literally dug up overnight on instructions from the Mayor. In another instance, one military officer endeavoured to use history in a defence of his squadron's operations. He responded to a noise complaint by sending a 1950s surveillance image of the complainants address asking him to mark his property on the photograph, stating "If you can show me your house, I'll tell my aircraft to stop flying over there!" It's a great story, but ultimately time marches on, as do the encroaching masses.

Perhaps some strength can be found in becoming a not-so-quiet minority. The headlines once heralded aviation, but maybe it is now our turn to do so. It is not a case of brandishing banners in the manner of our opponents, but highlighting the benefits of our endeavour to the greater community. Remind them of the airfield's application for aero-medical operations, or as the base for fire bombers and spotters. Open the doors to schools and community groups to visit the facility and re-generate the interest in aviation at a grass roots level. If the airfield possesses genuine historical significance, celebrate it. Erect a plinth, unveil a plaque and have community leaders and government representatives participate in the process. And make sure any of these positive events are covered by the media that is more often steered by those on the land-side of the airfield perimeter.

So often knowledge can dispel fear and we are the most informed individuals to do so. Interact and dispel the elitist myth, engage the community in a positive way; neither cowering nor confronting. Expand our horizons beyond like-minded individuals who already live in our comfort zones and endeavour to win over the fence-sitters. Our industry doesn't merely fly between capital cities. It provides a life-line to rural centres, generates income for the local economy and provides job opportunities; often without government funding. There are so many positives in aviation but they are unfortunately smothered by the recurring din of the vocal opponents.

Too many airfields live in the constant shadow of extinction. The arguments are so often unjust and ill-informed, yet they achieve their goal of rallying the troops while the developers are already drawing the runway and apron areas as a series of quarter-acre blocks. As the people who best understand our industry, it falls upon us to highlight its place in the modern community. It is time to take a proactive stance and share the benefits of aviation with the broader populous rather than simply waiting to repel the next adverse piece of publicity or development proposal.

We all share a passion of aviation for different reasons. It may be the sense of freedom, the history of those who have paved the way or the machines that lift us skyward. Whatever the motivation is, it is a common theme and no matter how magical the skies may be, ultimately we all need a place to land.

*****

48

Finding Amelia Earhart

Some time back, the headlines filled once more with the mystery of Amelia Earhart's disappearance and a new search for answers. No less than the, Hillary Clinton, highlighted the significance of the female aviation pioneer and her role as both a personal and national heroine. Ever since her disappearance in 1937 over the Pacific Ocean with her navigator, Fred Noonan, the story has bounced between a tale of tragedy and a conspiracy theory. Yet whichever path you choose to follow, the loss of Amelia is no less tragic or significant. Her story has inspired books, documentaries and feature films and today she is still a household name seven decades after her Lockheed Electra's engines went silent.

As we sit back in the flight levels approaching the speed of sound in air-conditioned comfort, it is almost impossible to grasp the enormity of the undertaking that Amelia was attempting when she vanished somewhere near Howland Island. Today, the smallest aircraft are equipped with crystal clear radios, reliable engines and even satellite navigation. The airways system has gone global and virtually anywhere, anytime someone else can know exactly where you are. In the era of Amelia Earhart, this was certainly not the case.

The pioneers at the dawn of air travel were virtually launching into the unknown. There were nautical charts and sextants to navigate by, while the likes of Bert Hinkler flew in his open-cockpit biplane with pages from the Times Atlas on his lap. They planned to the best of their ability, but the fact remained that the world had not yet geared up for aviation. There was no overnight courier to express-freight spare parts or weather radar iPhone Apps. It was a world of courage, initiative, determination and improvisation and to this backdrop they would take their small machines aloft over hostile mountains and miles of desolate ocean.

There were no creature comforts and hunger and fatigue were constant companions as the roaring engines deafened all on board. Both Amelia and Pacific crossing pioneer Sir Charles Kingsford Smith would send messages back to the crew on a stick as yelling against the engines' drone was absolutely pointless. All the while, the miles ticked by at a tediously slow rate in comparison to our modern world of the jet age. And so it is little wonder that many of these good people died forging the frontiers that we take for granted today.

Bert Hinkler would perish on an Italian mountain-side, while Kingsford Smith would be lost somewhere over the Bay of Bengal with only a lone undercarriage leg ever providing a silent testimony. Lancaster and Miller, Hitchcock and Anderson, Nungesser and Coli; the list goes on. Yet still these adventurers would seek to go farther, higher and faster without hesitation, well aware that the ultimate price could be there life. Amelia Earhart was one such heroine in a male-dominated realm.

Often these missions to find the answers to old mysteries give rise to detractors criticising the time, effort and cost that will be expended. However, if we are to inspire those in the future, we must continue to respect those who have gone before. For I suspect it is the same spark that inspires all heroes, regardless of their era. They are the same dreams that flow through the veins of an astronaut tethered in space as flowed through those who climbed aboard their machines of rag and tube a century ago.

As we search for answers to the challenges ahead for our world and its environment, once again it will be courage, initiative, determination and improvisation that will lead us to the answers. For at the heart of every solution is the human endeavour and it is that element that should drive the technology; not the other way around. The human spirit has survived through the most desperate times and hopefully it shall continue to do so. Yet to succeed we will need special people to forge frontiers where others will dare not tread. In these times we will continue to need our 'Amelias'.

So I shall continue to follow with interest as the survey crews and archaeologists pore over sonar plots and sift through the sand for clues. For even within the act of searching for Amelia there lies dreams, inspiration and hours of determined effort. The answer to Amelia Earhart's disappearance may well remain a mystery, but her spirit will only grow with time and therein lies the lesson for us all. Her success has not been lessened by her loss on that final leg across the Pacific Ocean, moreover it has emphasised that the true legend lies in the courage of the endeavour. Others subsequently built upon her efforts and ultimately the oceans and skies were traversed so that today we can bridge phenomenal distances with speed and safety.

Even in a world of split-second global technology, for us to successfully find our tomorrows, we need to keep looking for our Amelia Earhart's.

*****

49

When the Rain Comes Down

The sun is yet to rise and the rain is pelting down. Actually, to be more accurate it is thrashing the walls of my house, driven horizontally by howling winds. It's another half an hour before I have to throw my legs over the side of the bed and make my way to work, so I just lie there and listen to Mother Nature flexing her muscles. It's an awesome sound.

And it's a sound that has meant many different things to me over the years. As a young student pilot, each rain-drop carried a sting of disappointment as I knew that the flying lesson the next day was sure to be cancelled. The cloud base would be too low for stalling, or the crosswind too strong for circuits, either way it would be another frustrating day on Terra Firma. Even when the bonds of the circuit and training area had been broken, low pressure systems and developing troughs would destroy any chance of cross-country flying. If the weather was marginal, I would still venture out to the airfield and loiter around the briefing office reading the latest forecasts and bothering the 'Met Man' as if he could actually control the weather.

Sometimes I would be there for hours waiting for the weather to lift, only to travel home tired and disappointed. If only I'd really listened to that rain on the roof the night before.

Even my Commercial Pilot Licence flight test got underway five hours late because of the weather and in retrospect I was weary before the propeller ever turned. Still it was a great day that I'll never forget. Yet even when armed with a brand new CPL, the rain was still there to spoil the fun in other ways. Those early mornings, traipsing across sodden ground in the dark, up to my ankles in water as fresh drops ran down the back of my neck. Pre-flighting the aircraft outside amidst waves of falling water, only to take half the sea inside with me when I opened the cockpit door. I would then slide onto a wet seat with sodden socks and the peak of my cap dripping onto my already soaked flight plan and charts. Yelling "Clear Prop" at the top of my voice to make sure no-one else was stupid enough to be out in this weather and to highlight the fact that I was. With the engines started, there was a chance that the de-mister might actually clear the windscreen, but more likely it would turn my wet socks into boots of ice.

When I was fortunate enough to fly, I was then either dodging thunderstorms in Australia's vast north-west, or seeing flight lessons cancelled once again, but now as the instructor. An instrument rating brought some solace, but still no certainty. There would be days flying in the thin corridor between the lowest safe altitude above the terrain and just below the freezing level, which always seemed to get very narrow over the Great Dividing Range. Or those nights when the rain came by stealth in the form of ice, insidiously creeping along the wings and only exposed by the beam of my torch reaching beyond the cockpit. Some of those nights I was wishing that I was lying in bed listening to the rain thrash against the walls rather than buffeting me about the skies.

Even at the flight's end, the cloud maintained its mystery; how far down did it really extend? Would I be lucky tonight and see the ground? The lights of the land below would teasingly glow through thin breaks in the cloud before....yes...a glimpse...no...yes....that's it....definitely yes... the runway. VISUAL!!!! And still the rain would have the last word, smashing against the windscreen while the wind seemingly pulled the world sidewards. I would then do battle with the weather one last time to tie the aeroplane down and put her to bed. Believe it or not, I still look back on those dark wet nights with real joy and a sense of appreciation for the lessons that I learned.

Today, the world is a little different. I have two experienced pilots in air-conditioned comfort flying an aircraft with in-built redundancies of everything you can imagine. Turbine engines have replaced the pistons and anti-icing systems have proved far more effective than a torch. There are 'Head-Up Displays', flight management systems, RNP approaches and autopilots that actually work. Every few months there is simulator training to prepare you for the worst case scenario and every day wonderful cabin crew feed you when their workload permits. The rain and weather are still there, but these days experience, training and advanced equipment has provided me with the best set of defences that I can hope for. Regardless of whether it's a Beechcraft or a Boeing, it is still up to the pilot to recognise the variables that the weather inevitably brings and cater for them in the safest possible way.

It's now a little later, but it is still dark and wet. I am driving along the freeway with the wipers sweeping across my windscreen as fast as they will go. The wind is rocking the car and the steering wheel intermittently twists in my hand as the wheels strike a patch of standing water. I sit well below the speed limit and readily concede that this is the most dangerous part of my day as another numb-skull driver overtakes me at Mach Two. Then my memory trips back to another wet night and I'm just a boy lying in my single bed in our little fibro home in Sydney. It's 2am and the phone ringing has startled me at first and then I hear my Dad's lowered voice. There's the unmistakable rustling of his uniform shirt with its metal wings and plastic identity card and the steps of his undoubtedly highly polished boots. He has been called out on this foul night to guide his aerial ambulance to some remote township to help a stranger in need.

As the front door clicks shut, I hear him scamper through the rain to open our front gate. The rain is pelting down upon the roof and the wind is shaking the screen upon my window, but if I listen really closely, there's another sound. It's my father and he's whistling. It's 2am, it's pouring rain, he's about to launch into the night....and he's whistling. My head sinks back into my pillow and I think about my Dad whistling. And then I think about his job. There must be something to this pilot stuff. I might have to give it a go one day. Goodnight.

*****

50

Moments

In recent times I have had cause to both reflect upon and discuss what it is about aviation that attracts me and like-minded souls. It is a question that is inherently met with a reasonable pause before any sort of answer is forthcoming. Sentences often stumble and phrases falter in the search for the right words; it is like feeling one's way around a darkened room. Ultimately you make it to the other side in some sort of fashion, but it's neither efficient nor timely.

Much of this confusion stems from the juxtaposition of flight, for in so many ways it is where science collides with art. The rational, operational aspects can be strictly defined, published in manuals and committed to memory. However, the majesty of flight is far less easily captured. It is the sensations and emotions that are associated with this freedom in the three dimensions that can both captivate and confuse. And just like art, it can be in the eye of the beholder.

It is equally difficult to ask a purveyor of fine art why they like a certain work. They may wax lyrically about brush technique and the use of light, but struggle to define the quality that reaches into the heart and stirs their soul. It is intangible and unable to be quantified, but no less genuine than the paint, frame and canvas. And so it can be with aviation.

The most immediate sentiment expressed is often that of freedom. It is the ability to move freely in any direction and break the shackles of gravity and the earthbound asphalt. As long as man has envied the freedom of the birds, he was destined to be enthralled by it once he had mastered the skill of flight. And yet, when questioned more deeply, aviators will often drift away from the generalisations and grasp particular points in time when aviation took hold of their being with such a force that they can recall it in an instant. Perhaps the joy is not a painting but a puzzle in progress. Incomplete with pieces missing, but some small sections are already laid out in their rightful place.

As I reflect upon my own puzzle, I feel for the pieces one by one. The time when, as a very young boy, I sat beside my father and 'steered' an aircraft around the airfield with the 'steering wheel', while my father pushed the rudder pedals far beyond the reach of my short legs. The sound of the rushing air, which replaced the instructor's voice as I sat alone on downwind that very first time. Or that wonderful feeling on my first solo cross-country when everything was in order and I was able to sit up and breathe in the scenery like never before. The day over golden fields when the Mustang moved effortlessly through roll after roll and the scenery tumbled past the sky time and again. From the flight levels, the wonder of a rocket launch off the Californian coast that lit up the sky, just as dawn was breaking, while nature turned on a light show with its 'Southern Lights' as I steered back from Johannesburg. There are just so many.

Yet, on their own they are pieces of life's fabric, not an entire tapestry. That does not make them any less real or significant, just harder to put neatly into a concise package. Consequently, when aviators begin to express their passion they can be prone to ramble, leaping from experience to experience. For those who may not appreciate the art, the oration can be tedious and beyond comprehension, yet when in the company of their fellow pilots they will be surrounded by knowing nods and smiles of a shared experience. Their common language will draw forth more stories and often the hangar's candles will burn late into the night.

And from these exchanges, it is not only love stories that are written. Valuable lessons are learned and passed from one generation to another, be it the subtleties of a particular aircraft, or the early warning signs of nature's fury. Like the sailor's of old, much is to be gleaned from the first hand experiences of those who have gone before. The sea and skies can be angry, unforgiving places, but they can also offer glimpses into a world that those who are land-locked can only dream of.

The corner office is a treasured goal for many on the corporate ladder and yet as aviators sit aloft in their cockpits, the view from the office is ever-changing. Influenced by time, light, weather and a limitless list of factors, the earth below is an endless carpet. While the horizon functionally divides land from sky, it also provides the first glimpse of the day and the last settling rays of the evening in the most spectacular array of colours the eye will ever see. And the clouds that burble and build like uncontrolled froth from a coffee machine, or the low grey murk that merges with the hills and beckons the foolhardy.

251

All of this can be seen, not just in a lifetime, but in a day.

It is true; describing the special qualities of flight is not an easy task. It stirs something different in each of us and refuses to be categorised or labelled. Nor should words be able to adequately define such a sense of wonder. Where would the fun be in that? No, it is better to leave a little mystery, another stone unturned. A teasing thought that when the wheels leave the earth today, we might just see a sight that astounds us one more time. For as our log books fill with hour upon hour, it may well be the moments that truly count.

An impressive contrail as an aircraft ahead turns for home at the end of the day.

Dad.

One Last Word

Thank you for sharing my 50 tales of flight.

Hopefully these stories have cracked open the flight deck door, or allowed a glimpse inside the hangar that you may not have seen before. It has been my privilege to live a life amongst the clouds, but it is also my responsibility to share this wonderful world with others.

For now, I shall continue to fly and see the beauty in the people and the places I encounter. And I shall also continue to write of these special moments and share them with you. There is always fifty more tales to enjoy and more often than not, they find me. So I must depart.

Thanks again and safe flying.

Owen

***

Acknowledgements

First and foremost, I would like to thank my wonderful wife and tremendous children for their patience and support as I have ventured far and wide, only to return home and type away on the keyboard.

Thanks to my numerous magazine editors who have published my work over the years and continue to introduce me to new and exciting opportunities in the aviation world. A special thanks to the team at 'Australian Aviation' magazine; who have become more friends than colleagues over the years. Also, thanks to all of the generous contributors of images for this book including Seth Jaworski and Doreen McGlashan.

Thank you to all of my friends and fellow aviators for playing such a special role in this journey. And to my cherished mates who have left this life in pursuit of your passion; you will never be forgotten. To the war veterans who have shared their stories, the air crew who have shared the flight deck and the aviation enthusiasts who have shared their passion. Thank you.

Finally, a sincere thank you to my parents for their support of my dreams when that's all they were. In particular, my Dad, who took those dreams and turned them into reality with his guidance and seemingly endless patience and knowledge. I can only hope that I have grown into half the aviator he was.

***

Also by Owen Zupp.

"50 More Tales of Flight"

"Solo Flight" An Aviation Adventure.

"The Practical Pilot." A Pilot's Common Sense Guide to Safer Flying.

"Down to Earth" A Fighter Pilot's Experiences of surviving Dunkirk, the Battle of Britain, Dieppe and D-Day. (Grub Street Publishing. 2007)

Author's Website. www.owenzupp.com and www.thepilotsblog.com

Printed in Great Britain
by Amazon